STORIES FROM THE

Classical Ballet

BELINDA HOLLYER

WITH AN INTRODUCTION AND
PERFORMANCE NOTES BY

IRINA BARONOVA

AND ILLUSTRATIONS BY

SOPHY WILLIAMS

Macmillan Children's Books

IN LOVING MEMORY OF
TAMARA KARSAVINA

The author would like to thank Mr. Clement Crisp; Ms. Francesca
Franchi, the archivist at the Royal Opera House in London; and the staff
of the British Film Institute in London; for their help during the research
for this book.

Russian dates are given in New Style. The spelling of Russian names
translated from the Cyrillic script follows *Grove's Dictionary of Music and
Musicians*, except for names which are widely familiar in an earlier
translation form, such as Tchaikovsky and Nijinsky.

First published 1995 by Macmillan Children's Books
a division of Macmillan Publishers Limited
Cavaye Place, London SW10 9PG
and Basingstoke
Associated companies worldwide

ISBN 0 333 60818 6 (hardback)
ISBN 0 333 65259 2 (paperback)

1 3 5 7 9 8 6 4 2

A CIP catalogue record for this book is available
from the British Library

Printed in Great Britain

Contents

Foreword

THE best way to enjoy ballet is to see it performed. In a theatre you will experience the excitement of waiting for the house lights to go dark, for the orchestra to start playing, and for the curtain to rise on the stage. These days you can see some wonderful ballet on television and at the cinema but, however good the programmes are, nothing quite matches the zest of a live performance. This is partly because ballet is a performance art, and it needs an audience to give it life. If you are there, you are part of that performance. The dancers are not dancing for themselves: they are dancing to give you pleasure, to make you laugh or cry, to entertain you.

Every time a ballet is performed it is different from any other performance of the same ballet. Sometimes the differences are very small ones and the audience might not notice them – but the dancers know, for refining and developing the way they dance a role is a part of their art. Sometimes the differences are much more obvious ones. If you see two productions of *Swan Lake*, for instance, the styles of dancing may vary a lot, especially if two different ballet companies are involved. The choreography – the sequences of ballet steps which are created in harmony with the music – will have been adapted and altered; and the libretto – the story

– will have been interpreted differently. Sometimes even the music will have changed.

The eight stories in this book are classical ballet stories which are still danced all over the world. On stage, the stories are told without words through a combination of movement and music, based on years of training and technique, and on inspired artistic expression. It will help your enjoyment of a ballet to know the story in advance, and if you catch some of the flavour of ballet from these stories, you will also begin to understand something of its enduring magic.

BELINDA HOLLYER

Introduction

I WAS born in Russia, in the beautiful city of St. Petersburg, the home of the great Maryinsky Theatre and its famous Ballet Academy. But if it hadn't been for the Russian Revolution in 1917, I would never have become a ballerina.

My mother had terribly wanted to learn to dance, but she had not been allowed to: it wasn't thought proper by her family in those days. And I don't believe my own father would have approved if I had expressed a desire to go on the stage. So I would have grown up in the customs and traditions of the time, married a naval officer like my father, and led the life my family expected. But, in 1920, we had to flee from Russia. Eventually we reached Romania, and settled in miserable conditions in Bucharest.

When I was seven years old my mother took me to ballet classes, which were held by an ex-dancer from the Maryinsky Theatre in the small room where she lived. My poor mother had lost everything, and she and my father were having such a hard time, as all refugees do. I think my ballet classes were her way of coping; her way of achieving, through me, the dream that she had been denied.

I hated those classes! I couldn't understand why I had

to turn my legs and feet out, and climb on to the points of my toes in hard, peculiar-looking shoes. I had never been inside a theatre or seen a ballet performance, and so I couldn't imagine why I was being made to suffer the classes when I would much rather have been climbing trees in the factory yard where we were living.

But my mother was a very determined young woman. And I must have been good, despite myself, because the teacher eventually told my mother that we should try to move to Paris so that I could have ballet classes there. She said that I might turn out to be very good indeed, but she didn't know enough to help me, and that if I stayed with her she would ruin me. In later years, I have often blessed that teacher's wonderful honesty.

My father worked day and night to save enough money for the move. When I was nine we were finally able to go to Paris, and I was taken to meet Olga Preobrajenskaya. Madame Preobrajenskaya had not only been a very great ballerina with the Maryinsky Theatre before the Revolution, she was also the most wonderful teacher of the time. After a good look at me – and to my mother's joy – she accepted me into her school.

I found myself in a real dance studio, with proper *barres* to work at, and a mirror covering an entire wall. At first I felt shy because the other pupils were so self-assured and knew so much more than I did, but slowly I began to get interested, to like the classes, and to make friends.

One day I watched Tamara Toumanova, who was the

This is me when I was nine, in Paris. My ballet school put on a performance in aid of some Russian charities, and sixteen of us danced in it.

star pupil in my class, do some advanced double *fouettés*, and I thought they looked easy. But when I tried them myself I fell flat on my bottom! My pride was hurt, and I made up my mind to do everything that Tamara could do. I started to work with fierce determination, and soon I made good progress and started to develop a strong technique. Madame Preobrajenskaya also taught me to love the art of ballet – the art that she so magically passed on to her pupils.

I was eleven when I first performed professionally, dancing in a play for children at a theatre in Paris. Then the Paris Opéra invited me to dance in some special performances by young dancers. When I was twelve, George Balanchine came to watch the senior class at work, and chose me to dance in *Orpheus in the Underworld*, an operetta which he was staging in Paris. Each act had a beautiful ballet sequence, and Balanchine gave me a solo in the second act which was full of technical effects and always brought the house down.

Meanwhile, a new ballet company was being formed by Colonel de Basil, with George Balanchine as the choreographer. It was 1932, and the idea was to carry on where Serge Diaghilev had left off when he died, and so the new company was called, as Diaghilev's had been, the "Ballets Russes" – the Russian Ballet. Balanchine wanted some very young dancers to head the new company, and three of us were chosen: Tamara Toumanova, Tatiana Riabouchinska and me. We supplied youth while the rest

*I danced some wonderful roles during our first London season at
the Alhambra, when I was fourteen. On the left I am Princess Aurora in*
The Sleeping Beauty, *and on the right I am Odette in* Swan Lake.

of the company brought tradition and professionalism. We
knew how lucky we were to have such an opportunity, and
spring was in our hearts as well as in the air as we gathered
in Monte Carlo to begin rehearsals. A year later, during
our first London season, Arnold Haskell – the leading
critic of the time – nicknamed us the "three baby
ballerinas". The name stuck, and that's how we were
known from then on.

It was an extraordinary life for us, young teenagers in
a grown-up world: the "baby ballerinas" of a great ballet
company, perfoming in theatres throughout the world. But

we took it all in our stride, for all three of us were refugee children who had never known settled homes, and our new lives were very exciting; we all loved what we were doing. Our mothers travelled with us so we were all strictly chaperoned, and we were treated as children even though we were working as hard as the older dancers, and carrying the responsibility of leading roles. On stage, in our make-up and costumes, we looked much older than we were, and one young man in the orchestra kept looking at me during performances. Then he sent me a note to say that he'd like to meet me, and would wait at the stage door that night – I suppose he was going to invite me to supper. Imagine how he felt when I finally emerged: in ankle socks, no make-up, thirteen years old, and with my mother firmly in attendance! He stared at me in disbelief, went red in the face, and fled. I wasn't allowed boyfriends at all, and the first lipstick I ever used off-stage was one Alexandra Danilova gave me when I was fifteen. It was called "Tangee Natural" and it was very pale, or my mother would never have let me wear it.

George Balanchine soon left the company and we all missed him, but we worked instead with other wonderful choreographers such as Mikhail Fokine, Bronislava Nijinska and Leonid Massine, and our repertoire grew rich in new works as well as in the old classics. We danced all over Europe, in North and South America, and Australia and New Zealand. We visited places where ballet had never been seen before, and pioneered new ballet

You can see why people thought I was older than I really was – here I was only fifteen! We had just had a season in Hollywood, and I was trying to look glamorous in my first grown-up hat and coat.

Above left: *I created the role of the Queen of Shemakhan for Fokine's ballet,* Le Coq D'or. *Here we are in London, in 1937.*
Above right: *Me as Swanilda, in Act Two of* Coppélia. *I was dancing with the American Ballet Theater in Mexico City , in 1942.*

audiences. Some of our own people left the company to start schools and companies of their own. George Balanchine formed the New York City Ballet, where he became the guiding genius of a great company. And at the end of our Australian tour in 1939, Edouard Borovansky and his wife left to start a ballet school and then a ballet company in Melbourne, and their Borovansky Ballet was the vital first seed of today's National Australian Ballet.

I stopped dancing when I got married and had children. I was blessed with a wonderful husband and two

Présage *was a Massine ballet, danced to the music of Tchaikovsky's Fifth Symphony. This is from our Monte Carlo season in the spring of 1933.*

daughters and a son, and now also a beautiful granddaughter and a little grandson. They are the greatest treasures in my life: my family, my friends, my gang! But I have never stopped caring about ballet and dance. If I can give back to my art some of the happiness and learning it has given to me, by sharing it with today's young dancers, I shall feel satisfied. It's my way of saying thank you to the goddess of dance, who gave me so much. So now I visit schools in Britain and other countries for the Royal Academy of Dancing as one of their vice presidents; I give talks and advice to the students and teachers, and examine for scholarships. Sometimes, too, I am asked to coach leading dancers in the roles I have danced myself, and the ones that were created for me.

The best advice I can give you, if you are training to be a dancer, is to make sure you go to a very good teacher who will give you the right foundation on which to build. If you are not trained in the correct way it doesn't matter how much talent you have: you won't ever be able to achieve a strong technique, and you will be prone to bad injuries later on. If you have the right technical foundation, then you can develop artistry as well. No ballet class is just a physical workout; it's a mental and spiritual one too, and you should practise changing the feeling and the style of your movements according to the *enchaînements* your teacher sets you.

Ballet is a very fragile art form and yet it is very resilient. It has been kept alive, through triumphs and tragedies; by the great teachers, dancers and choreographers who have passed on their knowledge, experience and magic from one generation to the next. I hope this collection of classical ballet stories will go a little way to increasing your pleasure and understanding of their legacy.

IRINA BARONOVA

LA BAYADÈRE

The Temple Dancer

A ballet in three acts

Music by
LUDWIG MINKUS

Choreography by
MARIUS PETIPA
adapted by
NATALIA MAKAROVA

Scenario by
MARIUS PETIPA
and
SERGEI KHUDEKOV

This ballet was first performed at the Bolshoi Theatre in St. Petersburg on 4 February 1877. In the years that followed, many famous Russian ballerinas danced the role of Nikiya, including Anna Pavlova and Mathilde Kchessinska. The full-length ballet has been performed in Russia ever since, but it was not until 1961 that any of it was seen in the West, when the Kirov Ballet Company from St. Petersburg (then called Leningrad) performed just the 'Kingdom of the Shades' scene from Act Two. Years later the same scene was performed by the Royal Ballet in London under the instruction of Rudolf Nureyev, who danced the part of Solor himself. Margot Fonteyn danced the part of Nikiya.

In 1974, Natalia Makarova, who had trained and danced with the Kirov Ballet, staged the 'Kingdom of the Shades' scene with the American Ballet Theater in New York, and danced the part of Nikiya. Then, in 1980, the same company performed a revised version of the entire ballet – the first time it had ever been performed and presented in the West. Makarova danced the part of Nikiya, and Anthony Dowell danced the part of Solor. Now, *La Bayadère* is often performed in Western countries, as well as in Russia, although the versions are rather different.

SOLOR was the noblest warrior in all India. He was handsome and brave, and famous throughout the land for his skill and daring. But Solor had a secret which he kept locked in his heart – he was in love with a *bayadère*, a temple dancer, by the name of Nikiya.

This love, however, was without hope. All *bayadères*, when very young, were dedicated to the service of the gods for the rest of their lives. They lived in the Sacred Temple, set deep in the Sacred Forest, and spent their whole lives in the study of the intricate patterns and movements of the sacred dances, learning how to move with beauty and with grace, so they could honour the gods.

Nikiya was the loveliest dancer the temple had ever seen. When she danced, it was as if the air danced with her. Her body flowed from one movement to the next like water.

Solor had first seen Nikiya dance one day, long ago. While he had stood looking at her in wonder outside the Sacred Temple, she had paused in her dance. In that instant, as their eyes met, some part of his heart had leaped the space between them, and was hers for ever. And when Nikiya saw the young warrior standing in the forest clearing looking across at her, it was as if she recognized him, even though she had never seen him before. In the moment that Solor gave her part of his heart, Nikiya gave him her love in return. And once the love had been exchanged, there was nothing either of them could do to take it back.

From then on, Solor found reasons to pass by the Sacred Temple from time to time. It was a lucky day when he caught sight of Nikiya again, just by chance, and weeks passed before they found a way to meet. Solor had made friends with Magdaveya, a fakir who served at the temple, and Magdaveya helped him and Nikiya to steal what few moments they could together.

One day Solor returned to the Sacred Temple after months away in a far part of India. His companions had urged him to return with them to the city to celebrate the success of their hunt. But Solor had refused, and asked them to leave him to meditate before the Sacred Fire for a time. He hoped that he could find a way to talk to Nikiya, however briefly.

Solor's plan worked, for he caught sight of Magdaveya almost immediately. Solor glanced around quickly and then beckoned to him. Magdaveya agreed to look for Nikiya and tell her of Solor's arrival.

Just then, however, a procession of priests emerged from the temple, and Solor retreated to the edge of the clearing. The priests were led by the High Brahmin, and Solor realized that something important was about to happen.

Nikiya had been chosen as the leader of the *bayadères*, and today this was to be announced in a special ceremony. All the dancers were lovely; they would not otherwise have been chosen to serve the gods. But there was no mistaking Nikiya:

among the dancers, she was beyond compare. The High Brahmin had never seen her before – and all thoughts of his position disappeared as his heart filled with passion for the beautiful *bayadère*.

At the first opportunity, he took Nikiya to one side, and he told her so. The young dancer was deeply shocked, for to be loved by Solor, a warrior, was one thing – but the Brahmin was a man of God. The love of a High Brahmin for a woman was against all the laws she had ever understood, and Nikiya told him she could not accept his love. The High Brahmin was both hurt and angry, but he kept his grievance close to his heart.

When the ceremony was over, the dancers brought water to the fakirs. This was Magdaveya's moment, and he managed to whisper to Nikiya that Solor had returned and longed to see her again, if only for a few moments. It was unlucky that the High Brahmin was watching Nikiya when Magdaveya spoke to her, for her face lit up with happiness at the news, and although the Brahmin couldn't guess what had been said, he knew that no ordinary message had been given. He decided to watch Nikiya secretly, and see what happened next.

As soon as the clearing in front of the Sacred Temple was deserted, Nikiya slipped out of the temple. She danced with happiness as she waited for her lover to appear – and all the while the High Brahmin watched her from his hiding place. His heart burned with jealousy when he saw Solor arrive, and saw Nikiya run to throw her arms around him, laughing with delight.

Solor took Nikiya's hands in his, and looked at her tenderly. "I swear again, Nikiya, my love for you," he murmured. "I dedicate my love to you – look, I swear it by the Sacred Fire!" Together, the young lovers made an eternal pledge.

Suddenly Magdaveya returned, to tell them he thought they were being watched. "I haven't seen anyone," he explained nervously, "but I can feel danger around. You must leave now, Solor!"

As Solor disappeared into the forest, and Nikiya and Magdaveya slipped back into the temple, the High Brahmin fumed with rage at what he had seen. He, too, made a vow: a vow that he would destroy Solor.

Solor returned to the city to find a message from the Rajah awaiting him, announcing a ceremony at the palace to honour Solor's bravery and courage. At the height of the splendid festivities, the Rajah rose to speak. No one guessed what he had planned – that he had chosen Solor as a husband for his daughter, Gamzatti!

Solor was appalled. He had given his heart to Nikiya: how could he marry anyone else? But to refuse the Rajah was unthinkable. Anyway, it was already too late for Solor to think of excuses: the Rajah was already leading his daughter across the palace hall to present her to him.

The next moment Gamzatti was beside him; her veil was lifted by her proud father and she stood there in all her beauty, with her eyes modestly lowered. She was exquisite – Solor could see that. What could he do? He bowed before her; he took her hand and led her to the seats which had been prepared for them.

While the celebrations continued, the High Brahmin arrived for a private audience with the Rajah. In the madness of his passion for Nikiya, he had decided to tell the Rajah about Nikiya's and Solor's secret love, hoping that the Rajah would have his rival killed. But the Rajah had just named Solor as his daughter's husband in front of the entire Court, and had no intention of shaming her with such an action. He told the horrified High Brahmin that it would be much simpler to kill Nikiya!

Gamzatti overheard their conversation and decided to settle the matter herself. That evening, she summoned the *bayadère* to her rooms and, with a cold and menacing smile, offered her gold and jewels if only she would forsake Solor. Frightened, Nikiya tried to explain the love between her and Solor. "We are vowed to each other," she said. "Nothing can change that: I cannot stop loving him – and he will never stop loving me. He has sworn it!"

The Rajah's daughter had never been refused anything before, and she turned to Nikiya with a look of hatred. Nikiya, fearing for her life, drew a small dagger from her shawl to defend herself – but Gamzatti's attendant knocked it from her hand, and Nikiya fled back to the Sacred Temple, sobbing in despair. She knew she was powerless against the wealth and majesty of the Rajah and his daughter.

The betrothal ceremony of Solor and Gamzatti was the most magnificent in all India. Poor Nikiya had to dance at the court celebrations and, although she tried to move with her usual grace and charm, she was filled with sadness for the loss of her love, Solor.

Gamzatti and her father had made a wicked plan to kill the *bayadère* as she danced. After the first dance had finished,

Nikiya was presented with a basket of flowers and a message that Solor had sent them to her. Nikiya was delighted! Surely this sign from Solor told her that he had not betrayed her, after all? Filled with love and joy, she danced more beautifully than ever before, hugging the basket of flowers to her heart. But a poisonous snake was hidden amongst the flowers, and bit Nikiya. She staggered and crumpled helplessly to the floor. Solor didn't know that she had been poisoned but he saw she was dying, and something in him died as well: he sat as cold as a statue, unable to think or feel.

The High Brahmin rushed forward to offer Nikiya an antidote to the snake's poison. But as she watched the distant

figure of Solor being led away by the triumphant Rajah and his daughter, Nikiya's heart broke. She refused to take the antidote – she would rather die than live in such sorrow. Moments later, she lay dead in the High Brahmin's arms.

SOLOR was devastated by Nikiya's death. As his wedding to Gamzatti drew near, he became more and more depressed. His only thoughts were of his true love, Nikiya. Nothing – not even death – could part them now. When Magdaveya gave him opium to soothe his despair, Solor conjured up a vision of the Kingdom of the Shades – the spirit world where he believed he could find Nikiya and be with her once more. He searched through the misty kingdom, amongst the thronging spirits of the dead, until at last he found his *bayadère*. Reunited, they danced together with love and delight, as they had done in the forest clearing by the temple. But the vision was as insubstantial as the night, and faded from his grasp. The wretched Solor awoke to the realization it was the morning of his wedding to Gamzatti.

Solor's despair was complete. It was too late to change his mind, too late to find a solution to the terrible dilemma which confronted him. His head whirled with the opium smoke, and his mind was confused by his long nights of despair. Lost in a dream more misty than his vision had been, Solor found himself at the Sacred Temple, where the wedding ceremony was to take place.

Now that Nikiya was dead, Solor no longer cared what happened to him. Wearily, he let himself be lead through the complicated and lengthy ceremonies which would end in his marriage with Gamzatti.

Then, suddenly, he saw Nikiya: the vision from his dream had returned: she had not deserted him, after all! There she was, his glorious *bayadère*. She ran to his side, and then danced away again, her smiles encouraging him to follow her. No one else in the Sacred Temple could see Nikiya, and so they saw only that Solor seemed more distracted, and was behaving oddly. The wedding ceremony continued, but again and again Solor was diverted by the reappearance of Nikiya, who slipped between the living guests to lure Solor away with her.

The marriage ceremony was almost complete. As Gamzatti and Solor knelt before the High Brahmin, the bride gave her vow, and held out her hand. Solor did not move. The High Brahmin impatiently took Solor's hand and brought it down on top of Gamzatti's hand – they were now married!

At that very moment, a deafening clap of thunder shattered the silence. Everywhere was plunged into darkness.

Lightning flickered, and thunder boomed again. The temple walls trembled and, with a mighty roar, began to crumble around the heads of the horrified wedding guests. No one could escape. The Sacred Temple crashed to the ground, and everyone in it was destroyed. The gods, in fury, had spoken.

And in the Kingdom of the Shades, Solor's spirit joined Nikiya's. At last they could find rest and happiness together, united for ever in death.

IRINA BARONOVA'S PERFORMANCE NOTES

I heard about this ballet from my teacher in Paris, Olga Preobrajenskaya. She had been a great *prima ballerina* with the Maryinsky Theatre in St. Petersburg, and had danced the role of Nikiya many times. But, of course, I never danced it myself because no one in the West knew the whole ballet, so the choreography couldn't be re-created. The first time I saw any of it performed was that time when the Kirov Ballet Company danced the 'Kingdom of the Shades' on tour in London. It was stunning, and so simple. The whole *corps de ballet* – about forty dancers – appear one by one at the top of a ramp. Each one does an *arabesque penchée* followed by a back-bend, and then moves two steps forward to make room for the next dancer, and then the sequence is repeated: on and on they come, on down the ramp, another and then another, and you think there can't be any more, but there are. There's a lot of sparkling choreography throughout the ballet, with some terrific *pas de deux* for Solor with both Nikiya and Gamzatti. Maybe it's a bit of a museum piece, but it's very interesting.

Natalia Makarova has made an outstanding contribution to twentieth-century dance. In every way, she's been a great ballerina with complete artistry and finesse, who went on to adapt and re-create the choreography for this and other ballets as well. It was Makarova who put back the very last act of *La Bayadère*, which hadn't been performed since 1919. So she gave back to Petipa something of the legacy he had given her.

COPPÉLIA

The Girl with the Enamel Eyes

A ballet in three acts

Music by
LÉO DELIBES

Choreography by
ARTHUR SAINT-LÉON
and
MARIUS PETIPA

Libretto by
CHARLES NUITTER
and
ARTHUR SAINT-LÉON
based on a story by
ERNST HOFFMANN

This ballet was first produced at the Théâtre de l'Opéra in Paris, on 25 May 1870. It is based on a story written by Ernst Hoffmann, and the same story was used for the first act of an opera called *Tales of Hoffmann*, but there the doll is called Olympia instead of Coppélia. The musical score for *Coppélia* was written by Delibes, and it is famous for being one of the first in which special theme music is played whenever the different main characters come on to the stage.

The first ballerina to dance Swanilda was only sixteen years old, an Italian called Guiseppina Bozzacchi who had come to Paris in 1864 to study dancing. Her role in *Coppélia* was her dancing début, but after only eighteen performances of the ballet the Paris Opéra closed because the Franco-Prussian war was being fought and Paris was under siege. Thousands of Parisians died of hunger or typhoid during the siege, and Guiseppina Bozzacchi, too, died there on her seventeenth birthday, six months after her dancing triumph.

In the original French production, and in many subsequent revivals at the Paris Opéra, the part of Franz – the ballet's principal male role – was danced by a ballerina. Today, however, the best-known version of *Coppélia* is based on an 1884 production which was re-choreographed by Marius Petipa in St. Petersburg. In this, Franz is always danced by a man, and the choreography includes some *pas de deux* in which the dancer playing Franz lifts Swanilda in the air: something that a ballerina would find impossible.

ONCE upon a time, in a small country town in Galicia, there lived a strange old man called Dr. Coppélius. Some people thought he was a magician, and the children were rather frightened of him – but they still loved to peer into the windows of his tall, narrow house in the town's market square, trying to snatch a glimpse of the wonderful clockwork toys that Dr. Coppélius made in his famous workshop. However, Dr. Coppélius kept his shutters and curtains tightly closed, and his doors firmly locked.

Then, early one summer's morning, a curious thing happened. There, at the balcony window on the top floor of Dr. Coppélius' house, sat a beautiful young woman. No one had seen her before. She was delicate and lovely and she sat at the window with a shy and elegant grace, her eyes turned modestly down to the book she was reading. Everyone who saw her stopped to look at her in astonished admiration.

If they had only known the truth, they would have been even more surprised, for the beautiful girl was really a life-sized doll, made by Dr. Coppélius to trick the townspeople. He had named the doll Coppélia, after himself, and he had made her so cleverly that even he had begun to believe she was real. That morning he hid behind the balcony curtain so that he could watch the townspeople's reactions to Coppélia, and gloat at his own cleverness.

The first person to come into the square was a pretty young girl called Swanilda. She was always filled with fun and laughter, but today she walked in a dream, thinking about her sweetheart Franz. She almost missed looking up at Coppélia's window altogether, but as soon as she spotted the unfamiliar figure, Swanilda smiled a greeting, waved, and then called up to her.

"Good morning!" cried Swanilda cheerfully. "Are you visiting Dr. Coppélius? Why don't you come down and meet my friends?"

When Coppélia simply ignored her and continued to gaze at her book, Swanilda was offended. Indignantly, she turned to leave – but then she saw that Franz was following her into the square, and she decided to hide and watch his reaction to the beautiful stranger.

Sure enough – to Swanilda's dismay – Franz was spellbound. He bowed low to Coppélia and, glancing quickly around to make sure no one was watching him, blew a kiss up to the balcony.

At that very moment Dr. Coppélius decided he had had enough fun for the present, and he appeared beside Coppélia on the balcony, frowning fiercely in mock anger.

"How dare you address my daughter without an introduction?" he shouted. "Be off with you, at once!" With that, he wheeled Coppélia's chair out of sight, and firmly closed the shutters.

Swanilda had seen everything. Angrily, she challenged Franz to explain himself.

"It's you I love," Franz replied, a little impatiently. "Of course I don't love anyone else!"

When Swanilda still seemed doubtful, Franz felt a little angry himself. In his heart he knew he had been wrong to hurt Swanilda – he loved her dearly – but he only wanted to flirt for a while with the beautiful stranger. Surely that wasn't forbidden?

The square was beginning to fill with people, for it was time for the Mayor to make an important announcement. A new bell was to be hung in the church, and the lord of the manor wanted to celebrate by giving a bag of gold to every couple who was married in the church on that same day. Everyone was excited by this – Swanilda, however, wondered if she should marry Franz, as everyone expected. Did he really love her, as he said he did?

One of her friends handed Swanilda an ear of wheat fresh from the fields so that she could try out the "ear of wheat" test on Franz and his love. According to the test, if Swanilda shook the ear of wheat near her ear while she looked at Franz, and if he truly loved her, she would hear the wheat rustle. If the wheat kept silent, it was a sign that Franz didn't love her at all. At first Swanilda couldn't hear the wheat rustle at all; and when Franz tried to listen, he couldn't hear any sound either. One of their friends listened more carefully, and said the rustle *was* there, if you really tried to hear it.

By then, however, Swanilda had had enough! She threw the wheat away, and told Franz she wasn't going to marry him, after all. Refusing to stay in the square any longer, she ran off with three of her friends to talk about what had happened. The mysterious Coppélia seemed to have been forgotten by everyone.

When dusk fell, the square was deserted once more. Dr. Coppélius emerged from his house, dressed for his evening walk. After he had locked his front door with an enormous key, he set off across the square, using his umbrella as a walking stick to keep himself steady on the cobbles.

Dr. Coppélius was so deep in thought – planning more tricks to play with Coppélia – that the rowdy boys who had decided to tease him got exactly what they wanted! The old man jumped with surprise as they sprang from their hiding place, and in his startled fright he dropped his keys as he chased them away, hitting out at them

with his umbrella. Trembling with rage, Dr. Coppélius was rescued by an innkeeper who heard the commotion in the street, and invited him inside to recover.

In the meantime, the keys lay unnoticed in the square outside Coppélius' house, until Swanilda and her friends passed by on their way home.

"Look!" cried Swanilda in mischievous delight, her

troubles forgotten. "Dr. Coppélius must have dropped his house key – let's have a look inside."

Consumed by curiosity, her friends agreed. In a moment the key was turned in the lock, and with quick glances over their shoulders, the girls were inside the house.

Just as they disappeared, Franz crept into the square carrying a ladder – for he, too, was determined to solve the mystery of Coppélia, and had decided to climb up to the window where he had seen her to try to attract her attention. But Franz shrank back into the shadows as he saw Dr. Coppélius emerge from the inn across the street and start back towards his house. Franz would have to try again later.

MEANWHILE, Swanilda and her friends had cautiously made their way up the stairs to the very top of Dr. Coppélius' house, where Coppélia's balcony jutted out from the workshop. The big room was gloomy and dark when they tiptoed in, and inhabited by alarming life-size figures. Once they realized these figures were just mechanical toys Swanilda and her companions had a marvellous time. Laughing with excitement, they wound up the toys and watched them move, and pretended to be clockwork toys themselves.

Then Swanilda discovered Coppélia, hidden behind the balcony curtain. Her arms and face were as cold and hard as stone, her long-lashed enamel eyes were fixed in their stare, and no heart beat beneath the pretty dress she wore: Coppélia was just a beautiful doll!

An angry shout silenced their giggles. Returning from the inn, Dr. Coppélius had discovered his door wide open to the square. In a moment, he would climb the stairs and discover them.

Swanilda leaped to hide behind the balcony curtain where Coppélia was kept. Her friends were not so quick. While the furious old man chased her friends from the workshop, shouting and puffing behind them, the quick-thinking Swanilda changed dresses with the doll, hid Coppélia in a cupboard, and sat herself neatly in Coppélia's chair. Dr. Coppélius wasn't the only one who could play tricks, she thought to herself.

Poor Dr. Coppélius had only just returned to the workshop, panting from the chase, when there was yet another disturbance – this time at the window, as the besotted Franz appeared at the top of his ladder and cautiously climbed into the room.

"Just let me meet her," he begged – and, strangely, Dr. Coppélius agreed.

"Sit down and have a glass of wine with me, young man," he suggested, smiling oddly. "Then I'll show you anything you want." The cunning old man had quickly seen his chance. At last, he could try out a magic experiment he'd dreamed of performing for years . . . The drug in Franz's wine soon sent the young man into a deep sleep, and Dr. Coppélius searched through his books for the spell he needed – the one that would capture Franz's soul and transfer it to Coppélia's body, so giving her human life.

There it was! Dr. Coppélius held the book open and chanted the spell carefully over Franz, gesturing importantly at all the right places.

He wheeled Coppélia's chair out into the room, consulted

his book of spells again, and then waved his arms commandingly in the air. To his astonished delight Coppélia blinked when he blinked, shrugged her shoulders when he did, moved her arms stiffly, and then – oh, wonder of wonders! – she stood up.

"The spell has worked!" shouted Dr. Coppélius in excitement. Swanilda giggled silently. She was beginning to enjoy this! The doctor encouraged Coppélia to try out some simple dance steps. Her first movements were jerky and mechanical; she made sure she hit him with her stiffened arms as he moved clumsily around her. Then she gradually stopped moving, as though her winding up mechanism had run down. Dr. Coppélius' big moment had arrived: he would try and transfer Franz's soul into Coppélia's body.

As Dr. Coppélius continued to work his spell, his doll gradually seemed to lose her stiffness and began to take deep breaths. She seemed as delighted as he was that she had become human.

Coppélia smiled merrily and at first seemed willing to obey his instructions. But gradually, she became more and more out of control. Dr. Coppélius began to think that his doll was as awkward as a real human being. She played with the other dolls when Dr. Coppélius didn't want her to, and when he tried to stop her she mischievously chased him around the room with a soldier-toy's sword.

The tormented Dr. Coppélius couldn't understand what was wrong. Coppélia danced like a whirlwind, flying around the room in excitement.

She kicked the book of magic spells high into the air, and the pages fluttered apart in ruins to the horror of the confused doctor. And then, just as Dr. Coppélius found the lifeless body of the real Coppélia and realized that he had been tricked, Franz woke up from his drugged sleep and the two sweethearts escaped from the workshop, their differences forgotten.

WHEN the new bell was hung in the church, Swanilda and Franz led the couples who married that day. But when the Mayor presented a bag of gold to them Dr. Coppélius protested: after all the damage they'd done to his workshop! To show that they had forgiven him for his silly magic ideas, the young couple offered him their own bag of gold. The Mayor told them to keep it – and gave Dr. Coppélius one of his own, in compensation.

After that, everyone was happy. Swanilda and Franz danced and sang with their friends, and even Dr. Coppélius danced a little to show he had forgiven them.

IRINA BARONOVA'S
PERFORMANCE NOTES

I first danced Swanilda's role in *Coppélia* when I was in South America, performing as a guest artiste with Leonid Massine's ballet company. I had worked with Massine when he was a choreographer with Colonel de Basil's Ballets Russes, and so I was very pleased to dance with him when he had his own company.

Dancing Swanilda is exactly like going to a party! It's a gloriously happy ballet, filled with fun and laughter, and the role is a great pleasure for a ballerina to perform. You can enjoy the light-hearted silliness as Swanilda pretends to be a doll come to life: you can involve the audience in the fun as you turn away from Dr. Coppélius, and then compose your face in solemn stillness by the time you turn back to him. The acting is very straightforward, too – like the lovely moment when Swanilda, as the doll, first comes alive. Her blinking eyes and her first deep breaths are there in the music as well, so the joke can be heard as well as seen.

Being able to dance this role, as well as more serious ones like Odette-Odile in *Swan Lake*, is a great challenge for ballerinas. When you are a member of a touring company you might perform different ballets every night, for weeks on end. It's very interesting to dance *Coppélia* one night and a serious ballet the next – especially as the same people are often in the audience on both nights. If you could make them laugh out loud with Swanilda, and make them cry the next night with Odette, you felt enormous gratitude that your efforts to convey the roles, and make the audience believe you, had succeeded. It's as if you had been able to open a window on to a place of imagination and beauty and excitement.

THE FIREBIRD

L'Oiseau de Feu

A ballet in one act
of three scenes

Music by
IGOR STRAVINSKY

Choreography by
MIKHAIL FOKINE

Libretto by
MIKHAIL FOKINE
adapted from
Russian Folk Stories

This ballet was first performed by Diaghilev's Ballets Russes Company at the Théâtre de l'Opéra in Paris, on 25 June 1910. It was the first ballet music that Igor Stravinsky had ever written. He was only twenty-eight years old and his music was unknown in Western Europe, but Diaghilev encouraged new talent whenever he saw it. For *The Firebird* Fokine worked out the choreography section by section, miming the action while Stravinsky composed appropriate music at the piano.

Mikhail Fokine was one of the most important choreographers who ever worked in classical ballet. He not only created *The Firebird* and first danced the role of Ivan Tsarevich; he also created and danced many other ballets, formed and led his own dance companies, and did much to encourage the growth of ballet in the United States, through his work with de Basil's Ballets Russes and the American Ballet Theater.

In the first performance of *The Firebird*, the firebird's role was created by the great ballerina, Tamara Karsavina. Different versions of the ballet have been danced since then, all based on Fokine's original choreography. When Margot Fonteyn first danced the role in London in 1953, twenty-four years after Diaghilev died, Tamara Karsavina helped Fonteyn interpret the role as Fokine had taught it to her.

LONG, long ago, in the days when Russia was an uncharted land full of mystery, rich with great forests and plains that stretched further than you could see, and watched over by immense skies and long, silent, snowbound winters, there lived a handsome young man called Ivan. He was a Russian prince – a Tsarevich – and was the best hunter in all of Russia. He had tracked every animal that lived and every bird that flew across the vast plains and through the dark forests of his domains.

One day Ivan set out hunting before the dawn had broken. He wandered far from his usual paths, and, as the evening drew closer he found himself in an unknown part of the forest. The trees grew thick and close and seemed heavy with dark enchantment.

The courageous Tsarevich felt no fear. He moved quietly and cautiously through the trees, his bow raised in readiness, searching intently the shadows that enclosed him. He sensed that a mysterious prey was close by.

In the midst of this dense forest, Ivan came to a high wall which seemed to stretch for ever through the trees. In a moment he had scaled the wall, and dropped down on the other side into a beautiful garden. As the Tsarevich gazed about him in wonder, a shimmering light flashed across the darkening sky and danced through the air in front of him.

Prince Ivan ducked in surprise and fell back against the wall. What sort of creature could have brought the magical light with it?

With another surge of light, a fantastic creature burst through the air above him. It was a bird, yet more than a bird: an exotically beautiful woman-bird, filled with light and spangled with feathers of a fiery brilliance – a firebird. The Tsarevich watched in awe as the splendid creature flew through the air, flickering in the light which surrounded her. He drew in his breath in wonder as she alighted in the branches of an enormous tree covered with golden apples, and began to pick the fruit, darting from branch to branch in delight.

The young hunter could not see something as beautiful and strange as this firebird without wanting to possess it. He crept closer, making no sound, until he could see her more clearly. Then, with one lithe bound, he pounced. The firebird was his!

The terrified firebird struggled to free herself. A firebird cannot live in captivity: her flickering light and shimmering grace would grow dull with despair if she lost her freedom; and if she were caged, she would die. Prince Ivan held her firm, but she begged so eloquently for mercy, and pleaded with such urgency for his compassion, that the Tsarevich felt strangely moved. He had never before considered the feelings of any wild creature – indeed, it had never occurred to him that the creatures he hunted would have feelings that were worth his attention – but he had never met a firebird before.

Moved both by the firebird's beauty and her fear, Ivan

reluctantly loosened his grip. Sparkling in the shadows and as vivid as a flame, she danced through the garden, exalting in her rediscovered freedom.

In gratitude, the firebird plucked a brilliant red feather from her breast. It was a magic charm, she explained, and, if he was ever in trouble, he had only to wave the feather in the air and she would fly to his aid. The firebird leaped gloriously into the air again, hung poised for a moment, and then flashed off through the evening sky, with the prince running in pursuit, still transfixed in wonder at her beauty.

SOON, however, the firebird had left the Tsarevich far behind, and he returned to the part of the garden where the golden apple tree stood. Suddenly he heard voices and shrank back into the shadows beside the wall.

Ten lovely young girls ran into the garden, talking and laughing together. As they reached the garden they began to collect the golden apples and throw them to each other, all the while dancing and singing. The girls were so beautiful in their richly embroidered dresses, and they moved with such unusual grace and sang so sweetly that Ivan felt sure they were Russian princesses – Tsarevnas. But how could that be, and what were they doing here? Ivan sprang from his hiding place to confront them.

The Tsarevnas – for Ivan was right; these were princesses, not commonplace young women – shrank back at the sight of an intruder in their garden. How could this handsome young man have trespassed into their captive world? For the Tsarevnas were prisoners in their pretty garden: prisoners of the evil wizard Kostcheï, whose power over them and the garden and the forest around it was as absolute as it was fearful. Those who wandered into his domain were turned to stone: his palace and grounds were filled with the results of his malevolent magic. The princesses warned the young stranger he would be in terrible danger if he stayed.

Ivan ignored their warnings, however, for he had already fallen in love with one of the Tsarevnas, whose beauty had charmed him as soon as he had seen her. If he was in danger, what about the risk for her and her friends? Clearly, he must stay and try to rescue them from Kostcheï's power.

Ivan's courage won the heart of his Tsarevna. He bowed to her with dignified grace, and invited her to dance with him.

The other Tsarevnas joined in the dance, too, their evil master momentarily forgotten. They danced around the couple, now separating them, now reuniting them, in a circling dance that seemed to last for ever. And, while Ivan danced with her and watched her, his lovely Tsarevna seemed to grow in beauty and gracefulness as she swirled and clapped, smiling with delight. Perhaps, just perhaps, she might agree to marry him. Could he take her back to his own land as his bride? So Ivan dreamed as he danced through the darkening shadows of Kostcheï's enchanted garden.

A harsh trumpet call shattered their happiness. The Tsarevnas stopped their dance and huddled together. Ivan felt a stab of fear. Dozens of grotesque monsters had appeared as if from nowhere. With hideous features and misshapen bodies they surrounded the young prince, capering around him and taunting him with horrible laughs and cries.

Then, as suddenly as they had appeared, these creatures of darkness ceased their fearful dance and threw themselves to the ground around Ivan. Their master, the dread Kostcheï, had arrived.

He was a terrible figure, as if from a nightmare: his skeleton-body was hung with gaudy robes, his head covered by spikes of burning gold. He advanced on the helpless prince, his long nails clawing the air in an insatiable desire for his victim. A grin of insane delight contorted his features. There was no possible escape.

Ivan fumbled in his pocket for his hunting knife,

and as he grasped it his hand brushed against something soft and downy. The firebird's gift!

With a shout of triumph Ivan pulled the charmed feather from his pocket, held it high in the air, and ran among the startled monsters. The monsters snatched at him, but he evaded them all, laughing as he ran. Let them try to kill him now! He was invincible, with the firebird's help.

In vain, Kostcheï clawed at him, threatening and goading his monsters into greater efforts. The princesses bravely tried to plead for mercy, but Kostcheï ignored their entreaties. The intruder must be destroyed. He licked his lips and advanced again, weaving a terrible spell of destruction about him.

As Kostcheï prepared to pounce, a flash of light shot into the garden. The firebird! She darted among the monsters, bringing her fiery magic to the enchanted garden. As the firebird's spell began to work the monsters were caught up in a relentless dance: an infernal dance of unending movement. Their arms swirled and their feet thumped the ground, their legs writhed, and their hands clenched in time to a fearsome rhythm. They howled in fury, but they could not stop dancing; they swarmed and fell and were lifted into the air by an invisible force. Exhausted and reeling with dizziness, the monsters fell one by one to the ground.

The firebird danced again: a lullaby of a dance to soothe the monsters and send them to sleep. Even Kostcheï, the wizard, was unable to stay awake.

As soon as the garden was quiet and still, the firebird flew to where Ivan stood. "I have only enough power to keep them all asleep for a short time," she said. "You must search the roots of that hollow tree, where Kostcheï has hidden the enchanted egg which contains his soul. If you break the egg, Kostcheï will die and his wicked spells will be broken. But, oh, be quick, before he wakes!"

Ivan ran to the tree and dug furiously. He quickly uncovered a golden casket, richly encrusted with sparkling jewels. Inside was the egg: enormous, and as pale as moonlight.

The Tsarevich took the egg and raised it high above his head. As he did so, Kostcheï awoke; some suspicion of doom had proved stronger than the firebird's enchantment. The wizard saw Ivan holding his soul between his hands, and rose to his feet, shrieking with fear, but it was too late. Ivan brought the egg crashing to the ground, where it broke into a thousand pieces!

The garden was plunged into darkness. A whirling wind swept through it as Kostcheï's spell was broken. His reign of terror was ended for ever.

IVAN Tsarevich invited everyone to return with him to his palace, where preparations immediately began for his splendid wedding to the Tsarevna. Everyone in Prince Ivan's realm chanted and sang his praises, and told of his great deed in destroying the evil Kostcheï.

When at last the wedding day arrived, a magnificent procession lined the nave of the great cathedral, stretching all the way under the golden arches to the altar. The cathedral's bells rang as Ivan and his bride slowly made their way forward, carrying with them the blessings of all their people.

Ivan Tsarevich and his beautiful Tsarevna never forgot the firebird. Her generosity and courage had saved their lives, and released them from wickedness and the power of darkness to a life of light and beauty.

IRINA BARONOVA'S PERFORMANCE NOTES

When our Ballets Russes Company was touring America and reached New York, it was my turn to dance *The Firebird* on our first night at the Metropolitan Opera House. I felt so proud, and was determined to show New York how good we were.

When the firebird first appears she has a series of enormous leaps which carry her right across the stage, and then return her in the other direction. It's all in the music: you can hear the firebird being carried aloft in the way Stravinsky has written it. I started the great leaps across the stage in my beautiful firebird costume. But – disaster! My shoulder strap broke. One side of my costume started to fall down. Then, as I leaped back, the other strap broke, too.

Of course, there was nothing I could do: the firebird had to finish her *pas de deux* with Ivan Tsarevich, no matter what. Luckily, the bones in the bodice of my costume held it up, and so the whole top didn't slip right down, as I feared. It could have put me off entirely, but instead I was filled with a mixture of giggles and bravura – I was just determined that nothing would stop me. And so I think I danced better than ever before. But it was touch and go: I could have been the first ever firebird to appear topless!

Later, when I examined the costume, I discovered that the straps had been cut with a razor blade, leaving just a thread joining them up. Someone had been resentful that it was my turn to dance *The Firebird*, and had tried to spoil the evening for me. It was unheard of to have anyone behave so badly. In professional companies, people are usually very generous to each other and support each other's successes. Anyway, this bad trick was one that didn't work at all!

GISELLE

Les Wilis

A ballet in two acts

Music by
ADOLPHE ADAM

Choreography by
MARIUS PETIPA,
after
JULES PERROT
and
JEAN CORALLI

Libretto by
VERNOY DE SAINT-GEORGES,
THÉOPHILE GAUTIER
and
JEAN CORALLI
based on an idea by
HEINRICH HEINE

T his ballet was first performed at the Théâtre de l'Académie Royale de Musique in Paris, on 28 June 1841. It is probably the best-known classical ballet in the world, but it has quite a complicated history.

Giselle was performed for less than twenty years in Paris, and then it disappeared from the repertoire. No other company performed it in Europe, and the records of the ballet were lost in the archives in Paris. Luckily, however, the ballet had been performed at the Maryinsky Theatre in St. Petersburg. There, the great choreographer Marius Petipa produced his own version of the ballet – and that is the one we know today. When Diaghilev's Ballets Russes Company performed in Paris in 1910, they brought *Giselle* back with them to Europe from St. Petersburg: Tamara Karsavina and Vaslav Nijinsky danced it in Paris, for the first time in forty-four years.

At the première in Paris in 1841, Carlotta Grisi, an Italian guest artiste, danced the role of Giselle. Since then, almost every famous ballerina in the world has danced – or wants to dance – the role, and the shy young peasant girl has become an important landmark for ballerinas in the international ballet world.

O NCE, in a small village in Germany, on the edge of a grand Silesian estate, there lived a beautiful girl by the name of Giselle. Not only beautiful, but kind as well, the young girl enjoyed the love and protection of all the villagers. Giselle's mother cherished her only child, and took great care of her for her health was delicate.

Giselle's fragile beauty and loving nature gained her many admirers, and two young men in particular hoped to win both her heart and her hand in marriage. One was Hilarion, a local forester who had known Giselle all her life. The other was a mysterious young man called Loys, a newcomer to the village. The forester was jealous of the dashing Loys and the ease with which he seemed to have charmed his way into Giselle's affections. Hilarion suspected Loys of being more than he seemed, and kept a careful watch on him whenever he could.

The truth was more extraordinary than even Hilarion could have imagined. Loys was not a peasant at all, but Albrecht, Duke of Silesia. The young nobleman had seen Giselle in the forest one day and had fallen helplessly in love with her. He had come to the village to court her, disguised as a peasant, because he was afraid the beautiful young girl wouldn't take his love seriously if she knew his true identity.

Early one morning, Albrecht returned to the village from

a secret trip to his castle home. All was quiet and the village deserted, for almost everyone was hard at work harvesting grapes. Albrecht and his squire Wilfrid thought they were alone: neither noticed Hilarion hiding, watching them intently, his brow furrowed in thought: what was a peasant doing with a sword – and who was his finely dressed companion?

Wilfrid had always been uneasy about Albrecht's deception, and once more he pleaded with his master to return to the palace and forget about Giselle. But to no avail: Albrecht could not bring himself to abandon his love, nor yet to reveal his true identity to her. For the time being, he would have to remain disguised as Loys.

Leaving his cloak and sword in his cottage, the young duke dismissed his servant and went with a smile to knock on Giselle's door. Then, quickly, Albrecht hid from view. He knew that Giselle would be at home – for she was too delicate to work in the fields, and had learned instead to weave and spin – and he wanted to tease her a little.

Out peeped Giselle, remembering that Loys would return that day and eager to welcome her charming suitor. He must be hiding, she decided and, pretending not to care, she began to dance and hum to herself, all the while secretly trying to find out where Loys was.

She paused in her dance for a moment. She was sure she could hear a sound . . . Yes! From his hiding place, Loys was blowing her kisses! Giselle still couldn't see him, so she decided to pretend to sulk. That should do the trick. And, sure enough, as Giselle turned with a flounce to her cottage door, there was Loys beside her, smiling broadly and holding out his hands. Albrecht felt a rush of love at being close to his dear Giselle once more. Perhaps, after all, now *was* the right moment to declare his love for her?

He led the young girl to a bench beside the cottage. Taking her hand in his, Albrecht confessed his eternal love. "I swear that I love you; that I will always love you," he said softly. "Can I hope that you might love me, too?"

Giselle wanted to be completely sure of Loys' affections. Picking a daisy from the grass, she began airily to pluck the petals off, one at a time. "He loves me, he loves me not," she murmured, hardly daring to glance at Loys' face. "He loves me, he loves me not." As the last petal fell to the ground, Giselle burst into nervous tears. "He loves me not!" But Albrecht, picking up the flower, showed her that she had missed the last petal of all: one "he loves me" petal remained. Giselle beamed through her tears and began to dance once more, accompanied by the jubilant Albrecht.

From his hiding place, Hilarion had seen everything, and his heart burned in anger to see Giselle so happy with Loys. He leaped in front of them and wrenched them apart with a cry of rage. The startled Giselle frowned indignantly at Hilarion. "How dare you!" she exclaimed.

Crushed by her reproach, Hilarion fell clumsily to his knees. "My sweet Giselle," he begged, gazing up at her lovely face, "I'm the only one who truly loves you! Trust only me!"

But Giselle's patience was at an end. How dare Hilarion

embarrass her in this way? And he looked so foolish kneeling there, so unlike her dashing Loys. "I think you had better go, Hilarion. I have nothing more to say to you."

Hilarion stared up at her in dismay and pulled himself miserably to his feet. Filled with shame, the wretched forester rushed away. Loys held Giselle tenderly in his arms. He did love her: she was sure of that now. And she loved him, too.

By the time her friends returned from the vineyards laden down with baskets of grapes, Giselle's spirits had lifted. She joined her friends in their dancing and singing, and the sweethearts were a picture of happiness.

Her attention attracted by all the commotion, Giselle's mother glanced out of her window. Giselle! Dancing! She rushed to remonstrate with her daughter. Didn't Giselle remember that she was much too delicate to leap about? She should be resting more, and dancing less. Reluctantly, Giselle returned to her cottage with her mother, and one by one the villagers returned to their afternoon's work.

Hilarion returned to the village a few minutes later, still burning with anger at his rejection. He was determined to prove that his suspicions about Loys were correct. Suddenly he heard a hunting horn: a hunting party was approaching. He knew he must act quickly and slipped into Loys' cottage. "Perhaps," he thought, "I'll find some proof there that Loys has been lying."

The noble party entered the village, led by Wilfrid, Albrecht's squire. Unable to persuade the hunting party to choose another place to rest, he feared that Albrecht's identity would be discovered. But no: Albrecht was nowhere to be seen and Wilfrid breathed a sigh of relief.

The Prince of Courland and his daughter Bathilde, along with huntsmen and other members of the court, dismounted. Refreshments were needed, and now! Knowing no one else in the village would be at home, Wilfrid knocked with some trepidation at Giselle's door. As soon as her mother saw who had arrived she bustled around, preparing food and drink and setting up a table and chairs in the shade of a tree for the royal visitors.

Giselle's curiosity soon got the better of her shyness and it wasn't long before she joined in. A hunting party from the palace was too exciting to miss! Bathilde in particular was touched by Giselle's unaffected nature – and when she discovered that she and the peasant girl were both to marry soon, decided to give Giselle a present. After a quick word with her father Bathilde took a pretty necklace from around her own neck, and hung it around Giselle's. Giselle had never owned anything so beautiful, and she kissed Bathilde's hand in delighted gratitude. What a treasure to show Loys!

Bathilde decided to rest in Giselle's cottage for a time while the hunt continued. A hunting horn was left outside so that she could call when she was ready to join them. The hunting party departed and all was quiet again. Hilarion peered triumphantly from Loys' cottage. He had found the sword, and at last could show that Loys was not who he said he was. But hearing Giselle's friends returning from the vineyards, Hilarion hid. He wanted to choose his moment carefully.

The villagers persuaded Giselle's mother to allow her daughter to dance with them – "But only for a short while, mind you." Albrecht joined them, and the dance ended with the two lovers embracing, delighted to show their new-found love to all.

This was too much for Hilarion. He rushed from his hiding place, all thought of timing forgotten. Blind with rage, he thrust the sword into Giselle's startled grasp.

"There!" he shouted. "You see, Loys is not who he says he is; no ordinary man has a sword like this. Look at the crest on it. The same mark is on the hunting horn. He is an imposter!"

Giselle stepped back in shock. What could this mean? Why was Hilarion making such impossible accusations? What could cause him to invent such extraordinary lies? She stood shaking with disbelief.

But Hilarion persisted, too enraged to notice Giselle's distress. "The sword, Giselle, the sword!" he shouted. "Ask him about the sword!" He grabbed the hunting horn and blew long and loud. The hunting party would reveal the truth, he was certain of that.

Giselle moved hesitantly forward. "Loys," she asked in a trembling voice, "is Hilarion right? Does this belong to you? What are you doing with a nobleman's sword?" Albrecht did not reply, and Giselle's heart fell. There *was* something wrong, then, but what? She turned away with a sob.

Just at that moment, the hunting party arrived in the village clearing, thinking that Bathilde must have called them

back. Bathilde, hearing the confused noise, emerged from the cottage and stared, bewildered, at the scene before her. Who could have sounded the horn? And what on earth was *her* Albrecht doing here – and dressed in peasant clothes? The noble huntsmen stood in disbelief at the sight of their noble companion. Suddenly all became clear. Horrified, Giselle realized that her Loys and Bathilde's Albrecht were one and the same person. She had been betrayed!

Stricken with grief, Giselle tore Bathilde's necklace off, and hurled it to the ground. Everyone stood in silence, touched beyond words by her misery. Longing only for relief from the anguish in her heart, Giselle picked up Albrecht's discarded sword. She would kill herself! The horrified onlookers pulled the sword away. As if in a dream, Giselle began to dance again – the dance she had so delighted in with Loys just a short time ago. Her heart pounded, her vision blurred, her dance steps faltered. Swaying as if about to faint, she collapsed into her mother's arms.

Albrecht rushed forward but it was too late. Giselle was dying: the shock had been too much for her weak heart. Smiling lovingly at Albrecht, she softly breathed his name and reached up to touch his cheek. Even as she did so her hand faltered, and she fell back. Giselle was dead.

THE mournful ghosts of young girls who have been betrayed by their lovers and died before their wedding day, haunted the forest where Giselle lay buried. Any man who crossed their path between moonrise and sunrise was forced to dance with them – to dance until he died. This host of tormented ghosts was known as the Wilis, and stories of their dreadful power were whispered in fear throughout the countryside. No living man would freely choose to visit the forest graveyard in the Wilis' dark hours.

But late one night, Hilarion, driven by his grief, set out to find Giselle's grave. The graveyard clearing was filled with an eerie murmuring. Ghostly lights flickered and danced amongst the trees. The forester fled in panic, but the Wilis had sensed his presence, and began to gather.

As the moon rose, Myrtha, Queen of the Wilis, emerged to claim Giselle's soul. She summoned the spirits of the dead and they danced to her bidding: translucently beautiful in the moonlight, and terrifying in their pitiless obedience to their queen. Their dance over, the Wilis turned to face Giselle's grave. With a magic branch in her hand the Queen of the Wilis bent over the grave, murmuring a spell as she did so.

The earth silently parted, and suddenly Giselle herself stood there, veiled in white, her arms crossed on her breast, as they had been in death. Moving as though asleep, Giselle glided forward, and stood motionless as the Queen lifted the veil that shrouded her lovely head. Following the Queen's commands in a mirror-like trance, Giselle began to dance. The young girl's innocent spirit spun around and around, rejoicing in her liberation from the cold grave.

As suddenly as they had appeared the Wilis disappeared into the trees. They had sensed the arrival of a stranger. The sad Albrecht had come to lay white lilies beside Giselle's grave. Hanging his head in remorse, he remembered all that had been light and life to him so short a time ago.

There was a flicker of movement against the trees. Giselle? Albrecht shook his head in disbelief: surely he must have been mistaken. But no, there – again! It *was* Giselle! Leaping to his feet, the duke ran to join the shadowy figure dancing alluringly through the trees; she disappeared again, only to reappear behind him, and tap him softly on the shoulder in silent greeting. His heart leaped, and they danced together as they had so often before. And when the bewitched Giselle led her lover deeper and deeper into the forest, he willingly followed.

No sooner had the couple disappeared than the Wilis swept Hilarion back into the graveyard clearing. Exhausted, he begged for mercy, but none of the Wilis could feel compassion: they had no mercy to offer a man. They danced relentlessly, enclosing Hilarion and draining his strength still more. Helpless and broken, the forester was dragged inexorably to the lake. His fate was sealed. The Wilis danced in delight as he sank down into the lake and drowned.

When Giselle and Albrecht returned to the clearing there could be no escape for Albrecht either: it was his turn to die. Myrtha turned her cold gaze on him. Giselle's pleas were in vain: Albrecht must be danced to death.

Giselle's love for Albrecht, however, was as strong as the hatred that consumed the Wilis. Time and time again in the hours that followed she sought to save her lover. She was there, as lovely in spirit as she had been in life, offering Albrecht the strength he now so desperately needed. Each

time he fell exhausted to the ground, Giselle ran forward to urge him to his feet again.

Eventually, Albrecht could stand no more. It was Giselle's fate to join the Wilis: it was Albrecht's fate to die at their hands. It seemed nothing could save them now.

But salvation was at hand, for the dancing and pleading had taken them through to dawn – and with the dawn light came the waning of the power of the Wilis. As a far-off rooster crowed, Albrecht fell, exhausted but safe, to the ground. Giselle embraced him for one last time. As the Wilis vanished like mist back into the marshes from which they had risen, Giselle's spirit returned to the grave. Having saved her lover, Giselle could now rest in peace, no longer at the mercy of Myrtha's power. And Albrecht returned to the world, to live for ever more with the sadness of his lost love.

IRINA BARONOVA'S
PERFORMANCE NOTES

I never danced Giselle, although it's a fascinating role, and I dearly wanted to tackle it. But in the end I decided against it – and I still think my decision was right. My reasons were simple ones. Giselle's story is based on her fragility – both emotional and physical – and the ballerina has not only to act the part, but to look it, too. As with any role, you must, in fact, *become* Giselle, and not just pretend to be Giselle.

I knew that I could convey Giselle's emotional fragility, her naïve tenderness, her youthful shy joy at being in love, and her trusting heart. I knew I could handle her heartbroken discovery of Albrecht's betrayal, her mental breakdown, confusion and death. My problem was in Act Two. I could not match my knowledge of my own physique to my vision of Giselle, for in that part of the ballet Giselle must look fragile and ethereal – almost transparent – and I was not born that way! Alicia Markova had that wonderful quality and was superb; so was the Russian ballerina, Galina Ulanova. But when Anton Dolin persuaded me to rehearse the part with him, I would catch a glimpse of myself in the studio mirror and think: "You beastly girl, you aren't dead, you're not a ghost – I just don't *believe* you !" I was very much alive, and that quality showed in my every movement. I knew that no matter how hard I tried I couldn't alter how nature made me . . . and so I knew I couldn't be convincing as Giselle's ghost.

So remember, young readers, if you dream of going on the stage, always be honest with yourselves about any role. Do you understand it and feel it thoroughly? Do you look right for it? If not, you will never be convincing. And you will be a happier person and a better artist if you are truthful with yourself.

THE NUTCRACKER

Casse-Noisette

A ballet in two acts

Music by
PYOTR ILYICH TCHAIKOVSKY

Choreography by
MARIUS PETIPA
and
LEV IVANOV

Libretto by
MARIUS PETIPA
and
LEV IVANOV
from a story by
ERNST HOFFMANN

This ballet was first performed at the Maryinsky Theatre in St. Petersburg, on 18 December 1892. It was not seen in the West until 1934, when the Sadler's Wells Ballet Company presented it in London, with Alicia Markova as the Sugar Plum Fairy. Because it is set on Christmas Eve it has now become a favourite production for the Christmas holiday season with ballet companies throughout the world.

Children have always enjoyed this ballet – partly because Clara and Fritz and their friends are played by children. But the ballet story was never made completely clear, and in many Western productions, it became rather muddled. For years, some companies presented only Act Two, rather than the whole ballet, and there have been a lot of different versions of the story. In some of them the Nutcracker soldier turns into a handsome prince; in others he has two battles with the Mouse King, and doesn't finally kill him until he has begun his journey to the Land of Sweets.

In recent years, both the story and the ballet's production have been revised – first by George Balanchine in New York, and then by Rudolf Nureyev in London and Mikhail Baryshnikov in Washington. The story that follows is based on the libretto for those productions, and on Ernst Hoffmann's original story.

CLARA and her brother Fritz were almost bursting with excitement. It was Christmas Eve and the Christmas tree looked splendid, its branches laden down with sparkling lights and mysterious parcels.

The children's friends and their parents' guests were all thoroughly enjoying the Christmas party. And best of all, Clara's godfather, old Dr. Drosselmeyer, had yet to arrive – and he was bound to bring some wonderful presents for the two of them: he always did. Dr. Drosselmeyer was the very best godfather a child could wish for. His long years as a clockmaker had taught him all the secrets of making amazing mechanical toys, as well as clocks.

But there was a secret sadness in Dr. Drosselmeyer's past. Many years ago, he had been employed as a clockmaker in a royal palace plagued by an invasion of mice. None of the usual remedies had worked, and the palace had been in an uproar. The clever doctor had invented a mechanical trap, which had proved very successful – so successful, in fact, that half the mouse population in the palace had been caught.

The palace had been delighted – but the Mouse Queen had been furious. In retribution, she had cast a spell over Dr. Drosselmeyer's young nephew, and turned him into an ugly nutcracker doll. The spell was powerful, and complicated to break because there were two parts. Firstly, the nutcracker doll had to kill the Mouse King – an act of extraordinary bravery and daring for so small a toy, even though he was a soldier – and, secondly, a young girl must love him and care for him, despite his appearance.

Dr. Drosselmeyer had spent many years trying to break the spell, but to no avail. Now he had a new plan, and this year's Christmas party might just offer the opportunity he had been searching for. The old clockmaker knew his goddaughter was sweet and loving: if anyone could be kind to the ugly doll, it was Clara. Christmas Eve, too, seemed an excellent time to tempt out the Mouse King and his army, with all that good gingerbread and bowls of nuts lying around. Surely it was worth a try? So he set out for the party with a host of presents for the children, the nutcracker in his pocket, and great hope in his heart.

It was just after nine o'clock when he arrived. Clara and Fritz jumped up and down with anticipation – and they weren't disappointed. Their much-loved godfather produced their Christmas presents with a great flourish!

But when the clock struck ten the evening was suddenly over. Just when it had become really exciting! Clara began to cry with disappointment. The kind doctor took the sobbing child to one side. "Don't cry, my dear," he said. "Look, I have another present for you!" And he pulled the nutcracker doll from his pocket. Clara was enchanted, and she danced around the room with the nutcracker in her hands. Fritz watched his sister jealously. Why should *she* have an extra present, and not he? He snatched the nutcracker away, and

refused to give it back. Clara, furious, tried to take it – but her brother was too quick for her and threw the unfortunate doll across the room. When Clara ran to pick it up she found that her little soldier was broken.

It really was time for bed now! Reluctantly Clara and Fritz said goodnight to everyone. As she hugged her godfather, he whispered, "Don't worry, Clara, your nutcracker will soon get better." The remaining guests soon left, and the once-bright house was now dark. Only the lights on the Christmas tree still sparkled in the darkness.

When all was quiet and still, Clara crept downstairs. She

had resolved to take the poor nutcracker up to bed with her. Just because it wasn't handsome – and now was broken, too – didn't mean that Clara would forget it: her kind heart wouldn't let her do that. But where was the nutcracker? Ah, there it was! She sat down on the sofa and stroked it lovingly. She wouldn't go back to bed quite yet, she decided sleepily. Soon, she was fast asleep where she lay.

As Clara slept, Dr. Drosselmeyer slipped quietly back into the house. Glancing tenderly at his sleeping goddaughter, he retreated silently into the shadows of the room.

Clara suddenly sat up with a start. What was going on? The lights were flickering in a mysterious way, and the Christmas tree seemed to be growing bigger and bigger as she

watched, whilst the room faded away. Was she awake, or was she dreaming? And where had her nutcracker soldier gone?

There was a sudden noise in the quiet room, a flurry of movement in the stillness. Clara drew back in fright. Under the Christmas tree a fierce fight was raging: a whole army of ferocious-looking mice was pitched in battle against a host of toy soldiers. And who should be leading the outnumbered soldiers but Clara's very own nutcracker soldier! Clara blinked, and looked again. Surely she was dreaming . . . but no, it really was happening.

The fighting was intense. Swords flashed in the half-light. The Mouse King was beating the nutcracker soldier into a corner. Clara couldn't bear the thought of her poor

nutcracker being hurt again – and, with a loud cry, she took off her slipper and threw it at the Mouse King. It hit him on the head, and he staggered. As their king fell to the ground, the startled mice scattered in disarray, scampering back to their holes carrying the Mouse King's body.

The nutcracker soldier marched across the room. He had grown to full size now, and was almost as tall as a real soldier. In fact, he looked very handsome. "Thank you for saving my life and releasing me from the Mouse Queen's spell," he said graciously and bowed low in gratitude. As he spoke, the darkness began to lift – snowflakes fell delicately through the air, and a forest rose up out of nowhere. As a reward for their bravery, Dr. Drosselmeyer was sending Clara and his nephew on a fabulous journey, full of strange and magical delights.

THE King and Queen of Snow came forward to greet them, and to guide them through the forest to the Land of Sweets. As Clara gazed around, she realized that everywhere she looked were sweet delights: the snow was made from sugar, and the ice was spun candy! Every single thing had been created to enchant them – the trees, the royal palace in front of them, all were made from the food Clara loved most: gingerbread and nuts, chocolate and marzipan, ice cream and toffee!

In the royal palace of the Kingdom of Sweets, lavish celebrations had been arranged. A beautiful fairy greeted them, dressed in pink spun-sugar and wearing a sparkling iced-sugar crown. This was the Sugar Plum Fairy. She showed Clara to a throne made entirely from sweet things – and asked the members of the court to present their entertainments. First, some mechanical dolls performed a chocolate dance and then came a coffee dance, performed by two dolls in Arab costumes. Next came a funny tea dance by Chinese dolls, and finally there was a rousing Russian folk dance.

To Clara's astonishment, the next amusement was danced by flowers made from spun sugar! And then, the best part of all: the dance of the Sugar Plum Fairy and her prince. She was so lovely, her prince so handsome, and they moved with such joyous beauty and magic, that Clara was enchanted.

Then all the dancers joined together and whirled around and around in a fast-flowing shimmer of colour and light. As Clara watched, the lights grew dim and the music fainter . . .

. . . and she was back on the sofa, blinking and rubbing her eyes in astonishment. Was it all a magical dream? Clara smiled with pleasure as memories of the night's adventures came back to her, and the little girl drifted off to sleep again, wondering what had happened to her nutcracker soldier.

In the shadows at the back of the room, Dr. Drosselmeyer smiled with relief. The old man was exhausted from his efforts through the night: to protect Clara from harm and to break the spell, and then to make the reward as wonderful as possible. But had he *really* saved his nephew? He could only pray that it was so.

When the clockmaker finally arrived at his workshop, dawn was breaking on Christmas Day. There at the table sprawled the sleeping figure of his nephew – freed at last from the Mouse Queen's spell. It had not been a dream after all. His work was completed at last.

I R I N A   B A R O N O V A ' S
P E R F O R M A N C E   N O T E S

I learned something very important about ballet when Tamara Toumanova and I were rehearsing the Sugar Plum Fairy role, soon after we joined Colonel de Basil's Ballets Russes Company in Monte Carlo.

The whole system of dancing in Act Two is very pure and restrained, and very classical. When the Sugar Plum Fairy is dancing a *pas de deux* with her Prince, there's one part where she does *pirouettes* forward, quite slow and precise and separately spaced, and then her Prince lifts her up on to his shoulders.

Well, we baby ballerinas wanted to show how good we were, and so we decided we'd do two, four and six *pirouettes*, instead of one, two and three. Why not? We could do them, and there was time in the music to fit them in. But Boris Kochno, our Artistic Director, was a great librettist who'd worked with Diaghilev. When he saw what we were doing, he was furious. He explained that *The Nutcracker* was a delicate and elegant ballet; it was not a circus, or a backdrop for a piece of bravura and showing off. It was a classical ballet with a classical style, and if we interfered with that, we would spoil it.

So I learned that each ballet has its own special style, and that you have to dance each one in the way which belongs to it. You can't go putting your leg up behind your ear just because you can: it has to be right for the style and mood and taste of the whole creation you're a part of.

PETROUSHKA

A ballet in one act
of four scenes

Music by
IGOR STRAVINSKY

Choreography by
MIKHAIL FOKINE

Libretto by
IGOR STRAVINSKY
and
ALEXANDRE BENOIS

This ballet was first performed on 13 June 1911, at the Théâtre du Châtelet in Paris, by Diaghilev's Ballets Russes Company. Many people think this ballet was the greatest of all Diaghilev's masterpieces, and it certainly involved some of the finest talent that the ballet world has ever seen. Stravinsky wrote the music after the success of *The Firebird*, and worked again in partnership with Mikhail Fokine's choreography. The stage sets were designed by Alexandre Benois, who helped Stravinsky write the story, and who used his childhood memories of the Butter Week Fair in St. Petersburg. And two sensational ballet dancers, Vaslav Nijinsky and Tamara Karsavina, created the roles of Petroushka and the Ballerina.

Stravinsky began writing the music for *Petroushka* before he knew it would make a ballet but, of all his ballet music, this one most clearly tells a story with its sound: all the excitement of the fair dazzles your ear. Petroushka the Clown, the unhappy hero, is a well-known puppet character in Russia, but Stravinsky, Fokine and Benois gave him a new life and a new meaning.

IT HAD been a bitter winter in St. Petersburg that year: a time of numbing cold lasting for months on end. So everyone was delighted that it was almost Lent, and time for the Butter Week Fair again. The huge expanse of Admiralty Square in St. Petersburg was still covered with ice and snow, but for the next three days it would be a lively and crowded marketplace, packed with stalls and booths of every kind, and thronging with people: gypsies and peasants, noble folk and servants, little children and their grandparents, lovers and friends.

Everyone mingled together in the great open square. They wandered from booth to booth: trying something spicy from one of the street-pedlars' trays; having something hot to drink from one of the enormous samovars; riding on the merry-go-round – and all trying to keep warm in the frosty evening chill.

An organ-grinder and a dancing girl appeared, and for a while the crowd gathered around them, admiring the speed and skill of the girl as she whirled and spun in time to the music. Then a hurdy-gurdy was wheeled into the square, and another girl danced to that music, competing with the organ-grinder's dancer for the crowd's approval. Next, some coachmen danced a boisterous Russian folk dance, filled with shouts and swirling movement – and the crowd applauded wildly, enjoying every moment. What would they be offered next?

A roll of drums made their heads turn toward a blue-curtained stage. It was empty at first but, as everyone watched, a strangely dressed man appeared between the curtains and the crowd whispered in recognition, remembering that last year this Showman had produced great marvels for them. What would he do this time, they wondered, as they gazed in awe at his long dark robe, high-crowned hat and secretive face. They surged across to stand in front of the curtained stage, waiting expectantly.

As they watched, the Showman played a sweet melody on his flute. The sweetness of the melody contrasted sharply with the hidden bitterness of his nature. For the Showman used his powers cruelly: he mocked and tormented the creatures he controlled, compelling them to obey his every command. But the watching crowd were unaware of that – they just saw the marvellous show he presented.

The curtains slid slowly back to reveal three human-size puppets in open boxes. In the middle box stood a lovely Ballerina, with a perfect doll-like face, stiffly posed with her arms propped up and her head to one side, as if she were waiting to be wound up. In the box on the left stood a Moorish soldier, a dark and handsome figure, with a bright turban wrapped around his head, and wearing richly brocaded trousers and a bright silk tunic. A curved scimitar hung at his side, and his hands rested jauntily on his hips, ready for action.

On the other side of the Ballerina flopped a rag doll of a figure: Petroushka, the Clown. Dressed in a ruffled blouse and baggy trousers, he looked a perfect figure of fun, a limp and ridiculous figure. But Petroushka's heart was full of hope and love.

As the Showman's music changed its tune to the lively beat of a folk dance, the three puppets suddenly sprang into action. At first they danced on the spot, beating time faultlessly with the music, then they moved forward across the stage, a little jerkily but still perfectly co-ordinated.

The three dolls lined up along the front of the stage. The Moor and Petroushka danced in time with each other, jumping on the spot, while the Ballerina danced from one to the other, throwing kisses first to the Moor and then to Petroushka. Finally, as the music finished, the dolls ended their wonderful show sitting on the floor of the stage with their legs crossed, gazing out at the wondering audience. The puppets had ceased all movement, and were rigid and still once more. The show was over, for the present.

THE Showman kept his puppets locked away in cells behind the stage between performances. It gave pleasure to the Showman's evil nature to torment his creatures in private, as well as forcing them to display their skills in public.

Petroushka's cell had neither windows nor furniture. The only decoration was an enormous portrait of the Showman himself, looking mockingly down on his captive. Poor Petroushka believed he deserved better than the life he had been given, and he raged against the fate which had put him into the clutches of the Showman. The Showman might imprison him, but he could not stop him from loving the pretty Ballerina. Petroushka had resolved to protect her from the dangerous advances of the Moorish soldier who, Petroushka knew, didn't really care for her at all. And Petroushka was desperately jealous of the Moor.

The Clown's pale face was a mask of sorrow and longing as he paced his cell, beat on the door, and shook his fists in rage at the portrait of the Showman – the cause of all his unhappiness. Suddenly he saw the Ballerina, motionless, poised in the doorway of his cell. His heart's delight! Had she come because she preferred him to the Moor?

Petroushka's awkward clumsiness, as he danced for joy, capering around his cell, did little to impress the pouting Ballerina. She was too proud to sense Petroushka's honest heart and his true love for her. All she could see was a blundering Clown. "How ungainly, how vulgar!" said the Ballerina to herself as Petroushka redoubled his efforts to please her, leaping high in the air in a gawky show of delight. With a sniff of disdain and a swirl of her skirts, she turned on her heel and haughtily left.

Once again, Petroushka was thrown into despair. "Nothing will change," he thought wretchedly. "The Showman will always treat me as a mere puppet, and the Ballerina will never think of me as anything but a clumsy buffoon." Overcome with frustration, he took a run at the wall of his cell. His anger gave him a sudden burst of strength and, to his own surprise, he broke through the wall, collapsing in a heap half in and half out of the cell.

THE Moorish soldier, meantime, lounged happily in his cell – a complete contrast to Petroushka's prison. The Moor's walls were sumptuously decorated in vibrant colours, and the soldier, comfortable on his couch, played idly with a coconut.

The door opened, and there stood the Ballerina. She played a tune for herself on a little trumpet and danced delicately round the room. The Moorish soldier watched her with growing delight. What delicacy and beauty! He sprang to his feet and began to dance around the cell with her.

The foolish Ballerina lapped up the soldier's attention. She was so taken with the Moor's handsome appearance that she never dreamed what selfishness lay beneath. All he really cared about was his own comfort and happiness.

As they danced, the Ballerina rejoiced that her efforts to

charm him seemed so successful. Even when he stopped dancing with her and pulled her down to sit with him on his couch, the Ballerina only pretended to be shocked at this forwardness. Secretly, she was delighted.

At that moment, Petroushka forced his way clumsily into the room. He had managed to untangle himself from the hole in his cell wall, and had followed the Ballerina to the soldier's cell. When he saw them sitting happily together he was overcome with jealousy. In a furious rage, he confronted the Moorish soldier. The surprised Moor drew his sword and chased the Clown around the room. How dare this silly Clown interfere? He'd soon show him who was the stronger and braver of the two of them!

Petroushka dashed out of the door, escaping just before the Moor's sword descended on his head. "How brave and strong he is!" thought the impressionable Ballerina. Poor Petroushka had lost again.

OUTSIDE in the square, the fair continued late into the night. A group of nursemaids danced a folk dance, which set the crowd to roaring its approval. Then a dancing bear arrived with its trainer. Next, a dashing group of coachmen organized a dance, fast and furious and full of excitement. Soon the square seemed to be one mass of stamping, shouting, whirling colour. The snow began to fall, gently and steadily, but no one minded.

Strange noises were coming from the puppet theatre. As they grew louder, the crowd fell silent, and turned to see what was happening. Out from between the curtains ran Petroushka, trying to escape from the raging Moorish soldier, who darted out close behind him. As the Moor ran he flourished his sword above his head. Closely behind ran the Ballerina, secretly pleased that all the fuss was about her.

Petroushka panted as he ran, ducking and weaving as the soldier gained on him. The crowd was amazed. Could these figures truly be puppets, they asked each other? Who had ever seen puppets behaving like this before?

Stumbling and slipping on the snow, Petroushka sought to avoid the Moor's blows. Soon he could run no further: the Moor had cornered him, and raised his sword above his head. The crowd gasped, and the Moor brought his sword sharply down with a grunt of fury. Petroushka doubled up in agony. With one last valiant attempt to raise himself he fell back into the snow, dead.

The Ballerina and the Moor slipped away as the crowd gathered around Petroushka's body. A policeman was called to examine the body of the dead Clown. If it was a real person that lay there, a terrible crime had been committed. But the Showman appeared from the empty puppet theatre. Smiling reassuringly, he picked up the limp body of the Clown. Of course it was just a puppet, he said. "Look, see for yourselves, the body is made of wood and stuffed with sawdust!" And,

sure enough, a little trickle of sawdust poured on to the snow where Petroushka's body lay.

The policeman was satisfied, the crowd dispersed, and the snowy winter dark filled the square. The Showman stood alone in front of his puppet stage, holding Petroushka's body in one hand. He smiled triumphantly. He had fooled everyone, and Petroushka the puppet was dead.

Something made the Showman stop in his tracks, petrified. High above the puppet theatre, hovering in the night sky, floated Petroushka's spirit, shaking his fist menacingly at the Showman. He was free, free at last, to haunt his tormentor for ever. The Showman cowered, and staggered away in panic. The ghost of the dead Clown slumped gently forward on the roof of the theatre, his arms swinging gently, as the snow continued to fall on the now deserted square.

Irina Baronova's Performance Notes

De Basil's Ballets Russes Company was in Barcelona in 1935, playing at the Theatro Liceo, when we were asked to do a performance in Barcelona's bullring. It must have been for charity, I think. Anyway, we agreed, and a platform stage was built at one end of the vast circle of the bullring, and mirrors and tables were put into the plain cell-like rooms at the side where the matadors usually got dressed, so we could put our make-up on.

We were dancing *Les Sylphides*, *Petroushka* and *Le Beau Danube* that night. Posters advertising the big night had been put up all over Barcelona, and the bullring was packed: thousands of people had come. But most of them had never seen a ballet before, they were used to going to the bullring for the bullfights, and *Les Sylphides* was much too restrained and ethereal for them. So they were polite, but we didn't feel any enthusiasm from the huge crowd when we danced that ballet.

Then came *Petroushka*, and I was dancing the Ballerina in the usual costume of a crinoline dress, with long frilly pantaloons that went down to my ankles. We began well, but when I started to dance out of the box I felt the elastic in the waist of my pantaloons give way, and they started to slip down! I couldn't stop them, so I thought the best thing to do was to let them fall. I continued dancing as best I could with the pantaloons slipping – and when they had reached my ankles I danced my way out of them, picked them up on one foot, and kicked them away across the stage.

The crowd was delighted. This was more like it! They shouted *Olé*, they clapped and cheered, and the rest of the evening was a wild success.

THE SLEEPING BEAUTY

La Belle au Bois Dormant

A ballet in three acts,
with a prologue

Music by
PYOTR ILYICH TCHAIKOVSKY

Choreography by
MARIUS PETIPA

Libretto by
MARIUS PETIPA
and
IVAN VSEVOLOZHSKY
from a story by
CHARLES PERRAULT

This ballet was first performed at the Maryinsky Theatre in St. Petersburg, on 16 January 1890. Tchaikovsky was delighted to work on another ballet after *Swan Lake*, and Petipa gave him very detailed notes about his plans for the choreography, which Tchaikovsky used when he wrote the music. *The Sleeping Beauty* has now been a successful ballet for more than a hundred years, and the complete ballet has always been popular in Russia. In the West, however, audiences did not at first seem to like the full-length ballet, and so in 1922 Diaghilev's Ballets Russes Company presented a shortened version of the last act, called "Aurora's Wedding". When the Sadler's Wells Ballet Company reopened at the Royal Opera House in London in 1946, after World War II, they presented a revival of the complete ballet. It was a great success, and when the same company went to New York in 1949, they opened the season there with the complete *Sleeping Beauty*. Margot Fonteyn and Robert Helpmann danced the leading roles in both countries.

The ballerina who first danced the role of Princess Aurora in 1890 was Carlotta Brianza. At that first performance, Enrico Ceccetti danced both the part of Carabosse and that of the Bluebird – a combination of roles which would be very unusual today. A character role like Carabosse is usually played by a retired dancer, and when Diaghilev's Ballets Russes Company danced *The Sleeping Beauty* in London in 1921, Carlotta Brianza – who had been the first Princess Aurora thirty-one years before – played the part of Carabosse.

THE day that the baby princess was christened, King Florestan's court was dizzy with excitement and hectic, last-minute preparations.

Cattalabutte, the king's master of ceremonies, had checked every list and every task at least half a dozen times that morning. Perhaps, he thought, he should check once more that his all-important guest list was correct. The Lilac Fairy, the Fairies of the Crystal Fountain and the Enchanted Garden; the Fairies of the Woodland Glades, the Songbirds and the Golden Vine . . . yes, they were all on the guest list, thank goodness. If you left a powerful fairy out of something so important as a royal christening, you could be in very serious trouble indeed.

The preparations were complete. The baby princess lay in a cradle at the side of the hall, smiling happily under a richly decorated canopy, and ladies-in-waiting fluttered around the cradle in admiration. What an enchantingly lovely child the princess was, and what a pretty name had been chosen for her: Aurora.

"Let King Florestan know that we are ready to serve him," Cattalabutte declared. A fanfare of trumpets announced the entrance of the king and queen. There was no time left for worrying.

When the king and queen entered, the queen hurried to

the cradle, fondly kissed her baby daughter, and then rejoined her husband to mount the steps to their thrones. The trumpets flourished again, and Princess Aurora's six fairy godmothers entered in a glorious procession. Five fairies, attended by their maids of honour, led the way, followed by the most important fairy of all, the Lilac Fairy. She was accompanied by six grandly dressed cavaliers, bearing the christening gifts on silken cushions.

One by one the first five fairies danced enchantingly for the court, presented their gifts, and blessed the baby princess, predicting a long and happy life for their little goddaughter. Then it was the turn of the Lilac Fairy. Known throughout the kingdom for her sweet nature and loving kindness, she danced with a special grace and beauty: she was truly magnificent to behold.

The fairy dances and blessings completed, the court was ready for the christening party. But as the king and queen left their thrones to admire their daughter's fairy gifts, a sudden menacing rumble interrupted the joyous celebrations. Everyone turned to each other in alarm, and Cattalabutte remembered, with a jolt of fear, that there *was* another fairy godmother: the wicked fairy Carabosse. In forgetting to invite her to the christening, Cattalabutte had committed an unforgivable mistake.

Carabosse swept into the Great Hall in a black coach, drawn by enormous black rats. The court drew back in fear at this sinister figure dressed in a dark sweeping cloak and a sombre, ragged gown. She took a malevolent pleasure in their fear. Furious at having been forgotten, she was determined to make them pay for the insult. No matter that Cattalabutte prostrated himself before her, begging forgiveness: no matter that the king and queen pleaded for her understanding and compassion. Carabosse was bent on revenge. She turned in fury towards the cradle where the baby princess lay oblivious of the impending danger. The hag-like fairy raised her stick, and pointed it at the baby.

"Your daughter will certainly grow up to be beautiful, just as the other fairies have promised," she announced in a harsh, cracked voice. "She will be the most beautiful princess in the world. But then she will die! She will prick her finger on a spindle, and she – will – DIE!" And Carabosse whipped her great black cloak around her, shrieking with delight at the gasps of horror her curse provoked.

Distraught with grief, the queen wept inconsolably. The Lilac Fairy stepped forward to confront the gloating Carabosse. For a moment, the two fairies stood facing each other in silence, and then Carabosse turned away, satisfied that the Lilac Fairy could not erase her wickedness. But as she moved to depart, the Lilac Fairy, with great authority, commanded her to wait. Carabosse would have to hear what she had to say.

The Lilac Fairy knew that it was too late to cancel all the evil – but she could try to avert the worst of it. She stepped forward with her magic wand raised. Perhaps all was not lost after all!

"I cannot change everything that Carabosse has said," the

Lilac Fairy explained gently to the king and queen. "It is true that Aurora will grow to be beautiful. And it is true that she will prick her finger on a spindle – but she will not die. Aurora, and all the court with her, will sink into a deep sleep, a sleep that will last for a hundred years. A kiss from a handsome prince will bring the spell to an end."

The Lilac Fairy turned to Carabosse, who stood fuming, furious that her cruel plans had been thwarted, and ordered her to depart. As she left the Great Hall, everyone breathed a sigh of relief. The court rallied at the Lilac Fairy's reassuring words. After all, they could protect the princess – they could ensure that no spindles were ever allowed into the palace. They could turn the remains of the bad spell away from her, they were sure!

TWENTY years later, King Florestan's court was celebrating another happy day for Aurora: her birthday. She had grown up to be as beautiful as she was sweet natured. Her proud parents had ordered a splendid birthday party, and four princes had travelled great distances to the court to meet Princess Aurora, to try to win her hand in marriage.

Once again, Cattalabutte checked to see that all the preparations had been satisfactorily completed. Early that morning he had been horrified to discover a strange old woman spinning in a corner of the palace. She had scurried off just in time, thought Cattalabutte: if King Florestan had seen her with a spindle he would have ordered her immediate death.

It was time for the four princes to meet Princess Aurora and try to woo her. Each of the hopeful suitors danced with the lovely princess. She accepted their roses with a sweet smile – but none won her heart.

Suddenly, as if from nowhere, the strange old woman appeared again, holding her spindle out to the princess. Aurora was intrigued by this curious new toy: whatever could it be? Before anyone could stop her, Aurora smiled her thanks at the old woman – and reached out her hand for the spindle.

The young princess pulled back with a cry – the spindle's sharp point had drawn blood! It was just as Carabosse had predicted twenty years earlier . . . Swaying as if in a faint, Aurora crumpled to the ground. A piercing cackle silenced the court, and the old woman threw off her disguise: it was the evil fairy Carabosse herself. Her work done, she fled the palace, pursued by the king's armed guards.

"Don't despair, my dear," pleaded the king, trying to reassure his distraught wife. "Perhaps the Lilac Fairy's promise of protection will come to our help now." And, as he spoke, the Lilac Fairy appeared in the garden.

The princess would not die, promised the Lilac Fairy. This was just the beginning of the spell that would last for a hundred years. A strange peace fell on King Florestan's court. One by one, the courtiers went back inside the palace to prepare themselves for sleep. Then, as the fairy stood at the top of the steps holding out her wand, the spell began to work. The bright afternoon sunlight dimmed, and great trees rose magically from the ground to enclose the palace in their thick branches. The palace, and everyone in it, fell peacefully asleep.

ONE hundred years later, a handsome prince called Florimund was hunting with his friends in the forest. They arrived in a clearing overlooking a beautiful lake, some distance from where the enchanted palace still lay, suspended in time and undisturbed.

The hunting party decided to rest for a time and enjoy themselves. But the young prince felt strangely melancholy, and when everyone else was ready to hunt again he asked them to continue without him.

His friends gone, Prince Florimund wandered through the clearing and gazed out over the lake, deep in thought. To his astonishment, floating magically across the lake in a silvery boat, appeared the Lilac Fairy. She told the bewildered Florimund that he had been chosen for an extraordinary task. "In an enchanted castle, hidden from view for one hundred years, lies the Princess Aurora. She has been put under a powerful spell, and can only be woken by a kiss from a prince who loves her."

Florimund was intrigued by the Lilac Fairy's words. Could he see this enchanted princess? A fleeting vision passed before his eyes. Enraptured, the young prince begged to see more. Aurora's spirit danced into the clearing. The prince reached out to catch the spirit in his arms, but the Lilac Fairy stopped him. The vision would fade if touched. But Florimund could bear it no longer. He caught Aurora in his arms, and embraced her for the brief moment before she faded away.

"Where can I find her again?" implored Florimund, longing to be reunited with the princess. The Lilac Fairy gestured for him to board and sail across the lake with her. She would help him find Aurora and break the enchantment that bound her.

Carabosse appeared from nowhere to try to prevent the prince from leaving, but the Lilac Fairy's magic was too strong and Carabosse slunk away, finally defeated.

Florimund was amazed by the sleeping palace. A vast impenetrable web of trees and creeping vines held it captive; the air was hushed and still. With the help of the Lilac Fairy, Florimund made his way through a maze of high columns to where Aurora lay peacefully sleeping on a silken bed canopied with lace and draped in cobwebs and dust.

Florimund bent over the bed and gazed longingly at Aurora's lovely face. She was even more beautiful than the vision the Lilac Fairy had shown him. A faint smile stirred at the corners of her mouth as if she were enjoying a delightful, sunlit dream. The prince kissed her gently on the lips – and there was a sudden flash of light. The spell was broken!

As Prince Florimund gathered the princess in his arms the cobwebs fell away, light flooded into the long-darkened castle, and the guards and pages stirred from their posts. The court of King Florestan had awoken from its enchanted sleep.

At the wedding of Florimund and Aurora the court was as happy and bright as it had ever been. Many special guests had been invited – characters from fairytales such as Puss-in-Boots and Beauty and the Beast were all there to wish them a fortunate life. The Bluebird of Happiness came to

dance for Aurora, for the princess' release from the spell was the happiest occasion possible.

Finally, the happy couple, Prince Florimund and Princess Aurora, danced together, too, and everyone in the Great Hall fell silent as they watched. The court knew that their princess would leave them now, to return with her husband to his kingdom, and so there was a note of sadness mixed with their joy. But they knew that all would be well now that the spell was ended, and a new life had begun for everyone.

Irina Baronova's Performance Notes

One of the most famous parts of Princess Aurora's role in this ballet is the "Rose adagio": the dance in Act Two where Aurora meets her foreign suitors, dances with each of them in turn, and each of them gives her a rose. The music is lovely, and it's delicious to dance, although it's quite tricky technically at the beginning because Aurora is left *en pointe*, in attitude, and unsupported as each suitor in turn approaches her and takes her hand to kiss it. The ballerina has to have very good balance and a strong back to hold her position successfully, without wobbling.

The "Rose adagio" was missing from the ballet when I danced it in the 1930s, because we were using a shortened version. But then, to my pleasure, Anton Dolin put it back into the choreography when he and I were working with the American Ballet Theater in the 1940s. So I was the first ballerina to dance the "Rose adagio" for an American audience.

The other lovely role for a ballerina in this ballet is the Lilac Fairy, who has some wonderful solos to dance. She also has some important mime to perform, which has to be done in a very clear and dramatic way, so that the story is understood. When you mime something on stage you have to convey the meaning through the words in your head. It all has to be thought out in separate silent sentences matched to separate clearly made gestures, so that the audience can follow what you are saying. It's so important to get the timing right – just as it is with any sort of acting. Any artistry has to be built on a combination of thought and technique, and good mime is an example of that.

SWAN LAKE

Le Lac des Cygnes

A ballet in four acts

Music by
PYOTR ILYICH TCHAIKOVSKY

Choreography by
MARIUS PETIPA
and
LEV IVANOV

Scenario by
VASILY GELSTER
and
VLADIMIR BEGITCHEV
adapted from
European Folk Stories

The original *Swan Lake* was first performed at the Imperial Bolshoi Theatre in Moscow, on 4 March 1877. Tchaikovsky had composed the wonderful music, but the choreography was not successful, and the ballet seems to have been rather a disappointment. It was not until eighteen years later, when Marius Petipa and Lev Ivanov presented a revised *Swan Lake* in St. Petersburg, using Tchaikovsky's music but adding their own choreography, that the ballet became a huge success. This version – on which all modern productions are based – was first performed at the Maryinsky Theatre in St. Petersburg on 27 January 1895. Pierina Legnani, one of only two dancers who ever held the official title of *prima ballerina assoluta*, created the dual role of Odette-Odile. Sadly, Tchaikovsky was dead by then, and he could never have guessed how famous his first ballet would become.

Since that St. Petersburg première, *Swan Lake* has never really left the stage. Sometimes just Act Two is presented, but today it is almost always the full-length ballet that audiences demand. In 1934, the complete ballet was performed for the first time in London, with Alicia Markova and Anton Dolin in the leading roles. In 1949, the Sadler's Wells Ballet Company took the complete *Swan Lake* to New York, where Margot Fonteyn danced Odette-Odile.

The greatest ballerinas of pre-revolutionary Russia, such as Mathilde Kchessinska, Olga Preobrajenskaya, Anna Pavlova and Tamara Karsavina all wanted to dance the dual role of Odette-Odile. Today's ballerinas feel the same, and modern productions also make the role of Prince Siegfried a brilliant and challenging part for men. All leading classical dancers want to dance *Swan Lake* at least once in their careers, for the choreography represents the sort of challenge that a Shakespearean play does to a classical actor.

PRINCE Siegfried had been looking forward to his twenty-first birthday celebrations for months and now, at last, they had begun. He and his friends had been invited to attend some entertainments just outside the palace grounds, devised by local villagers.

The villagers were waiting excitedly when the palace party arrived. Some of the young girls gave flowers to Siegfried and others helped to fix the maypole in place, while Siegfried smiled his thanks and offered drinks to everyone. Then the dancing began, with group after group eager to show what they had prepared for the royal party. Siegfried and his friends enjoyed themselves enormously. His old tutor, and one or two of his friends, had rather too much to drink, and when Siegfried's mother arrived, it reminded her of what she must say to her son.

"Now that you have come of age," she said firmly, "I expect you to take life a little more seriously. You must find a suitable bride: the future queen." Siegfried tried to make light of it, for he had no desire to marry – but his mother persisted.

"At the ball tomorrow night," she reminded him, "will be the six most eligible young women in the kingdom. All you have to do is to choose one of them to be your bride." And then, with a further icy glance of disapproval at the drinkers, Siegfried's mother swept back into the palace grounds.

The villagers were still dancing, but Siegfried's good humour had disappeared. He hated the idea of an arranged marriage and his mother's determination made him uneasy. His friends tried to distract him, but although he rejoined the celebrations, the young prince's unhappiness persisted.

By now, dusk had fallen. His friend Benno glanced up at the evening sky and saw a flight of swans passing overhead on their way to the forest, their great wings beating in unison. "Look!" he shouted. "Let's get together a hunting party and follow those swans!"

Siegfried's spirits were immediately raised, and the young men, armed with crossbows, hurried off after the swans.

THE great lake shimmered in the moonlight, unruffled by even the faintest breeze. A ruined chapel stood on the shore, from which an evil spirit in the form of a great owl surveyed its dominions. Hearing the hunting party, it slunk back to hide in the depths of its lair.

Siegfried's friends had run ahead of him, and continued along the side of the lake. As soon as they had left the clearing, Siegfried arrived – and, with a rush of wings, so did the swans.

Excited, Siegfried knelt beside the lake, his crossbow at the ready. As he watched, one of the swans alighted on the ground beside the ruined chapel. It seemed not to be a swan at all. Was it a woman or a bird who stood there, with such fragile grace and beauty? A woman surely, for her slender body was that of a young girl – but the beautiful face was framed by swan feathers, and her pale dress was soft with swansdown. As Siegfried watched, the wondrous creature bent her head so that her cheek touched her shoulder, just as a swan might preen its feathers. The moonlight, breaking through the clouds, glittered on a delicate lacy crown nestled in her hair.

Siegfried advanced softly, but his movement caught her eye, and she froze in shock. Her body quivered in terror and her arms beat the air frantically like a swan's wings. The hunter begged her not to fly away, but the swan-woman looked at the crossbow which he still held. Shuddering with fear, she asked if he intended to kill her.

Already in love, Siegfried swore that he would never dream of harming her; he implored her to stay and talk to him. Accepting the prince's word, the beautiful swan-woman agreed.

Her name, she explained, was Odette, Queen of the Swans. She had not always been a Swan Queen, but had been bewitched by an evil spirit. All her mother's tears, which now filled the lake before them, had not moved the evil spirit to compassion. His magic had condemned Odette to be a swan, except between midnight and dawn, when she was permitted to regain her human form. The swans who flew with her were swan-maidens too, under the same extraordinary enchantment. And a swan she would always be – unless a man swore to love her, married her, and never loved another. Then she would be released from the swan-magic for ever.

"I will release you from this evil spell," declared Siegfried, "for I will always love you. I will marry you, and never love another. Dearest Odette, come away with me now!"

Just at that moment the evil spirit emerged, sensing a threat to his wicked enchantments. His owl face was beaked and dangerous, and his talon-like hands stretched out to Odette, ordering her to return to his side. With a defiant shout, Siegfried lunged for his crossbow. Standing tall in the moonlight, fearless in his anger, Siegfried took careful aim. Let the evil spirit die at his hand!

But Odette ran to put herself between the crossbow's aim and the owl-sorcerer's menacing figure. "If you kill him, I too will die! Only after the spell is broken will I be safe from harm."

Siegfried lowered his crossbow; the sorcerer vanished, and Odette fell thankfully into her lover's arms. "Come to the palace tomorrow night, for my birthday ball," begged the prince. "I am supposed to choose a bride – and I will choose you, in front of all the world"

But Odette was too frightened of the sorcerer's powers. "If I tried," she murmured, "he would stop at nothing to spoil your plans and make you break your promise, Siegfried. Then I will be a swan for ever!"

As they talked, another danger threatened – for Siegfried's hunting companions had discovered Odette's swan-maidens, and in the soft moonlight thought they had tracked down the swans they intended to kill. Odette ran to safeguard them. If they tried to kill her maidens, they would have to kill her first! When Siegfried explained, the huntsmen suddenly saw the swan-maidens more clearly, and bowed humbly before the lovely creatures.

As the first streaks of dawn approached the shore, Odette had no choice but to return to the lake with her swan-maidens. She held out her arms longingly to Siegfried; but her feet carried her irresistibly back to the lake, where the swans waited beating their wings, and the cruel-beaked owl hovered, reclaiming his victims.

THE next night, the palace was filled with glittering excitement and glamorous figures – for everyone of any importance in the kingdom had gathered to celebrate Prince Siegfried's birthday. What a party it was to be!

Siegfried, however, found it hard to attend to what was happening, and impossible to enjoy himself. All he could think of was the night before, and his meeting with the beautiful Swan Queen. How he longed to be at her side, rather than at this party! Try as he might to be polite to his guests, his thoughts kept returning to the lakeside, and to Odette and her maidens.

Cross that her son should seem so distracted and inattentive, Siegfried's mother drew his attention to the six beautiful princesses just entering the room. They bowed gracefully to the prince and his mother, and then danced a stately waltz together.

Siegfried descended from his throne to the ballroom floor as though he were in a dream. Solemnly, he took the hand of each of the six princesses in turn, and led her in a dance while the whole room watched, eager to see which of the six he would choose. "How strange!" the courtiers murmured to each other as they watched: the prince didn't seem interested in any of the princesses. Although he was courteous to each, none seemed to warrant a second glance from him. What on earth could be wrong? Was he ill?

The prince's mother grew angry with embarrassment. She thanked the bewildered young princesses for their elegant dance and congratulated them on their beauty, doing her best to smooth over the awkward situation. Then she turned to her son. "Which one will you choose?" she demanded. The room grew quiet in anticipation.

"These princesses are indeed lovely," replied Siegfried coldly to his mother, "but I will marry none of them, mother, for I love another. I will marry no one but her!" And, bowing low to the princesses, he turned to gaze out of the window, his thoughts lost in the night.

A trumpet blast broke the scandalized silence. A herald

ran in and conferred with the prince's mother, for an unknown couple had arrived and, although he didn't have their names on his guest list, they seemed very grand. Should he allow them entry? Impatiently, the Queen agreed: any distraction would be welcome at this stage.

To a crash of cymbals and a flickering of the lights the doors flew open, and the strange couple entered the room. The man was a tall, bearded knight who called himself Von Rotbart. He introduced his daughter, Odile, to Siegfried and his mother, bowing low before he glanced up and fixed the prince with strangely glittering eyes.

The prince was beside himself with excitement. Looking at Odile, the prince thought he saw his heart's desire, his beloved Odette. He did not see that the coldly beautiful woman who stood haughtily in front of him was returning his passionate gaze with icy calculation. For Odile was the sorcerer's daughter, and Von Rotbart was the sorcerer himself. He had bewitched Siegfried, so that the prince saw and believed only what the evil spirit wanted him to, and nothing else.

The real Odette beat her arm-wings against the great windows of the ballroom – but in vain. Siegfried was spellbound. He rose from his throne, descended the steps, and stood before Odile. As he looked deep into her cold black eyes, the vision of Odette drew back from the window, exhausted. Only a single swan's feather remained for a moment, and then sank like a breath of air to the ground.

Siegfried escorted Odile into the garden, gazing at her

with delight: his swan princess was at his side, and all was well. Now the evil Von Rotbart turned his charm on Siegfried's mother, and she, beguiled by his magic, invited him to sit by her side. Who was this man? Could his daughter be a suitable match for her son? Really, she must find out more . . .

The entertainment began again, with renewed energy. Everything was sparkle and delight again, and when Von Rotbart suggested that Siegfried and Odile might dance together, Siegfried's mother graciously agreed.

Siegfried danced as if in a dream. Dazzled by his love, he did not see that the real Odette had returned to the ballroom window once more. Odette knew that if the evil spirit could trick Siegfried into betraying her – to say that he loved Odile and would marry her – then the prince would have broken his promise to her, and she would be a swan for ever. She beat against the window with her feathery arms, crying in a silent agony of despair.

Her movements caught Von Rotbart's eye. He moved between the window and the prince, smiling as he did so. With Odile's claw-like hand in his, Siegfried led her across the room to her father.

"I want to marry your daughter," he said to Von Rotbart. And wondered why the room had gone dark, just for a heartbeat.

Von Rotbart smiled his assent, and turned to Siegfried's mother: she smiled her assent in return. But Von Rotbart needed to be quite, quite sure he had won.

"Will you love my daughter for ever? Swear you will!" he demanded, watching the prince closely through narrowed eyes. "Swear you will never love another!"

Siegfried blinked to steady his head; he felt a confused echo of another time, another promise. But when he looked at Odile, his head cleared miraculously. Of course, that was why he had heard the echo of his promise. His beloved was by his side!

"I swear it!" he cried into the darkening echo of the room, as with a shriek of triumph, the spirit revealed himself and his daughter as their true selves. In a moment, Siegfried

realized what he had done, and turning away in horror he finally saw Odette fluttering hopelessly at the window. He rushed from the ballroom with a cry of grief, but Odette had vanished. The prince ran through the dark forest to the lake, fighting against a gathering storm, hoping against hope that he could find Odette again, and somehow put right the terrible wrong he had done.

THE swan-maidens had gathered at the lake to comfort their grief-stricken queen. "I have been betrayed," she sobbed, "and so I must be a swan for ever; for ever in his power. The evil spirit has won." But the swans urged her to wait for Siegfried's arrival.

"You know it wasn't his fault," they pleaded. "How could a human have withstood the evil spirit's enchantment? How could Siegfried have known he was under a spell?"

Frantic with sorrow, the prince staggered into the clearing. He searched in growing panic amongst the maidens. Their compassion finally overcame them, and they parted to reveal Odette hidden amongst them.

Siegfried begged Odette for her forgiveness, and out of love she gave it to him, weeping for their lost life together. Only death could free her now from the owl-spirit's power.

With a crash of thunder, the evil spirit appeared, exulting

in his triumph. He taunted Siegfried with the reminder that he had sworn to marry Odile, and of the consequences of his promise. At his command, the swan-maidens danced in the moonlight, unable to resist or to deny his will.

Odette knew that she must die. With a last loving embrace, she left Siegfried's side and ran towards the lake, to throw herself into its depths. And Siegfried, unable to imagine life without his beloved Odette, realized that he, too, must join her.

Thunder and lightning ripped through the sky as the evil spirit tried to stop the lovers, for he knew that his power would be destroyed by their death: his evil could not withstand such perfect love. But he could not stop them. As they sank beneath the waves, cradled in each other's arms, the evil spirit crumpled to the ground, an empty bundle of feathers. His evil reign was over.

The swan-maidens watched from the shore as Odette and Siegfried sailed away to another world. Nothing could separate them now; never again would unhappiness touch the beautiful queen and her loving prince.

Irina Baronova's
Performance Notes

I was fourteen when I first danced the dual role of Odette-Odile in *Swan Lake*. Colonel de Basil's Ballets Russes Company was performing in London. I had never danced the role before, of course: it belonged to the senior ballerina of the company, Alexandra Danilova. But I had watched from the wings every night it was performed, and I had stayed behind at rehearsals to see it rehearsed, so I knew the ballet well.

Danilova became ill in London, and it was clear that she wouldn't be well enough to dance in *Swan Lake* the next night. There was no time to change it for another ballet, so Colonel de Basil said that I was to dance it!

But the male dancer who would have partnered Danilova thought it was beneath his dignity to dance with a fourteen-year-old – and he refused rehearse the ballet with me. De Basil was furious and I was in tears, a soon there was a full Russian drama going on, with everyone shouting and nobody listening. And then Anton Dolin walked into the room. He was a guest artiste with the company, and already one of the most famous dancers in the world. When he heard what was wrong he smiled at me, and then he said that he would dance *Swan Lake* with me, himself! He spent the rest of that day and all the next coaching me in the role.

The audience was wonderful, and I could hardly believe my luck, that at last I had danced *Swan Lake*. But the most exciting moment of all for me was when Anton Dolin turned to me during the curtain calls, and kissed my hand. I didn't wash that hand for two weeks, I was so overcome! But Dolin was always so generous and wonderfully kind to young dancers; he never suffered from a moment's jealousy or an inflated sense of his own importance.